HAL•LEONARD

ESSENTIAL SONGS



PIANO VOCAL GUITAR

# Christmas Carols



ISBN 978-1-4234-8251-2

7777 W. BLUEMOUND RD. P.O. BOX 13819 MILWAUKEE, WI 53213

In Australia contact:
**Hal Leonard Australia Pty. Ltd.**
4 Lentara Court
Cheltenham, Victoria, 3192 Australia
Email: ausadmin@halleonard.com.au



line at
**www.halleon m**

# CONTENTS

# ALL MY HEART THIS NIGHT REJOICES

Words by PAUL GERHARDT
Translated by CATHERINE WINKWORTH
Traditional Music

# AS EACH HAPPY CHRISTMAS

Traditional

# ANGELS FROM THE REALMS OF GLORY

Words by JAMES MONTGOMERY
Music by HENRY T. SMART

C7 F Dm C/E Dm/F Am G7 C
Come and wor - ship! Wor - ship Christ, the new - born King! Sag - es, leave your
C/G G7 C F C Am G7 C
con - tem - pla - tions, Bright - er vi - sions beam a - far. Seek the great De -
C/G G7 C E Am E7 Am G/D D7 G G7
sire of na - tions; Ye have seen His natal star. Come and wor - ship!
C7 F Dm C/E Dm/F D7/F♯ Gsus G7 C
3fr
Come and wor - ship! Wor - ship Christ, the new - born King!

# ANGELS WE HAVE HEARD ON HIGH

Traditional French Carol
Translated by JAMES CHADWICK

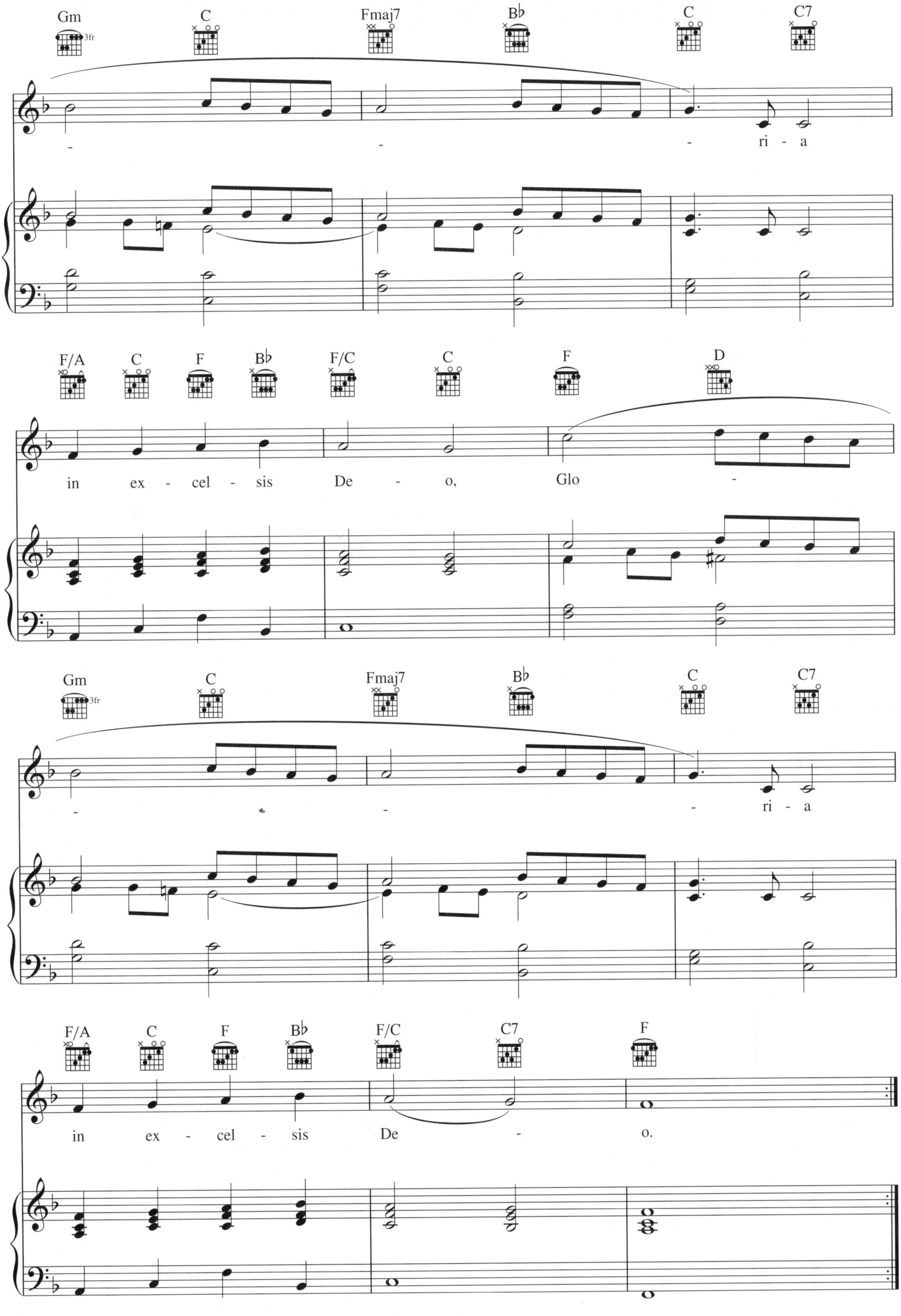
Gm C Fmaj7 B♭ C C7
3fr
- - - ri - a
F/A C F B♭ F/C C F D
in ex - cel - sis De - o, Glo -
Gm C Fmaj7 B♭ C C7
3fr
- - - ri - a
F/A C F B♭ F/C C7 F
in ex - cel - sis De - o.

# AS LATELY WE WATCHED

19th Century Austrian Carol

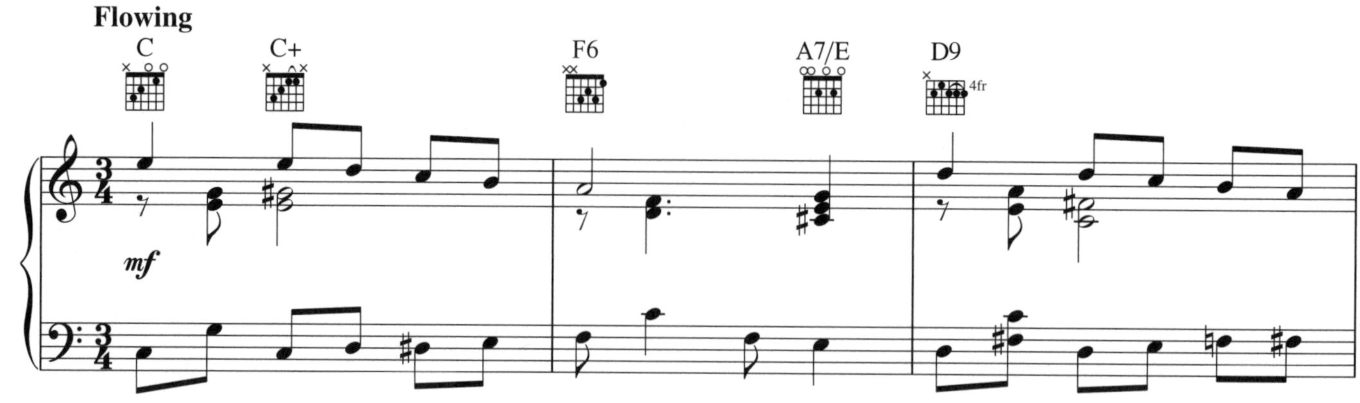

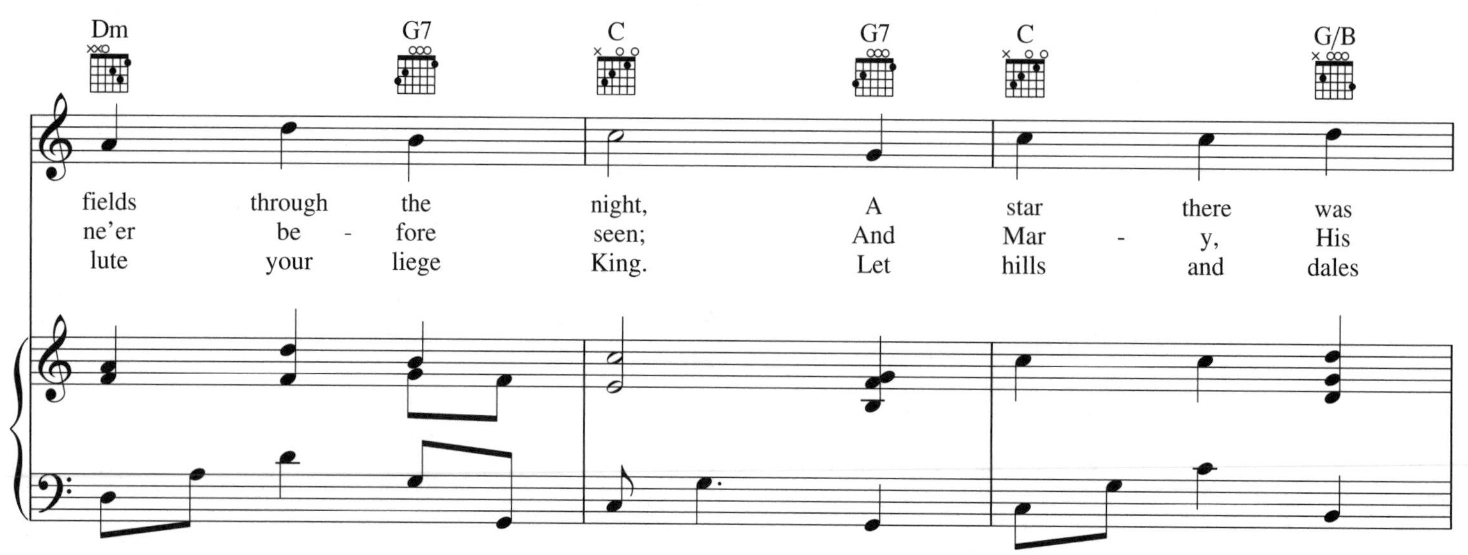

Am
Dm
G7
C
seen of such glo - ri - ous light!
Moth - er, so like to a queen.
ring to the song that ye sing.
C+
F6
A7/E
D9
4fr
All through the night an - gels did
Blest be the hour, wel - come the
Blest be the hour, wel - come the
G7
C
G/B
Am
sing, In car - ols so sweet of the
morn, For Christ, our dear Sav - ior on
morn, For Christ, our dear Sav - ior on
Dm
G7
1, 2
C
G7
3
C
C6/9
birth of a King. A
earth now is born. Then
earth now is born.

# AS WITH GLADNESS MEN OF OLD

Words by WILLIAM CHATTERTON DIX
Music by CONRAD KOCHER

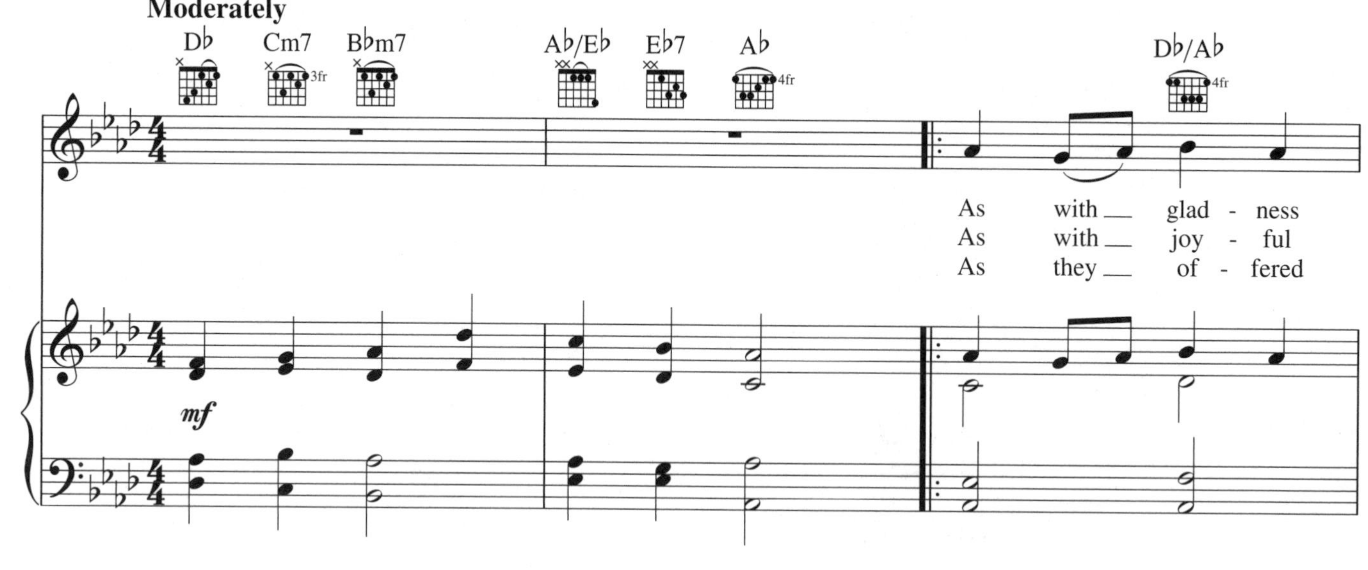


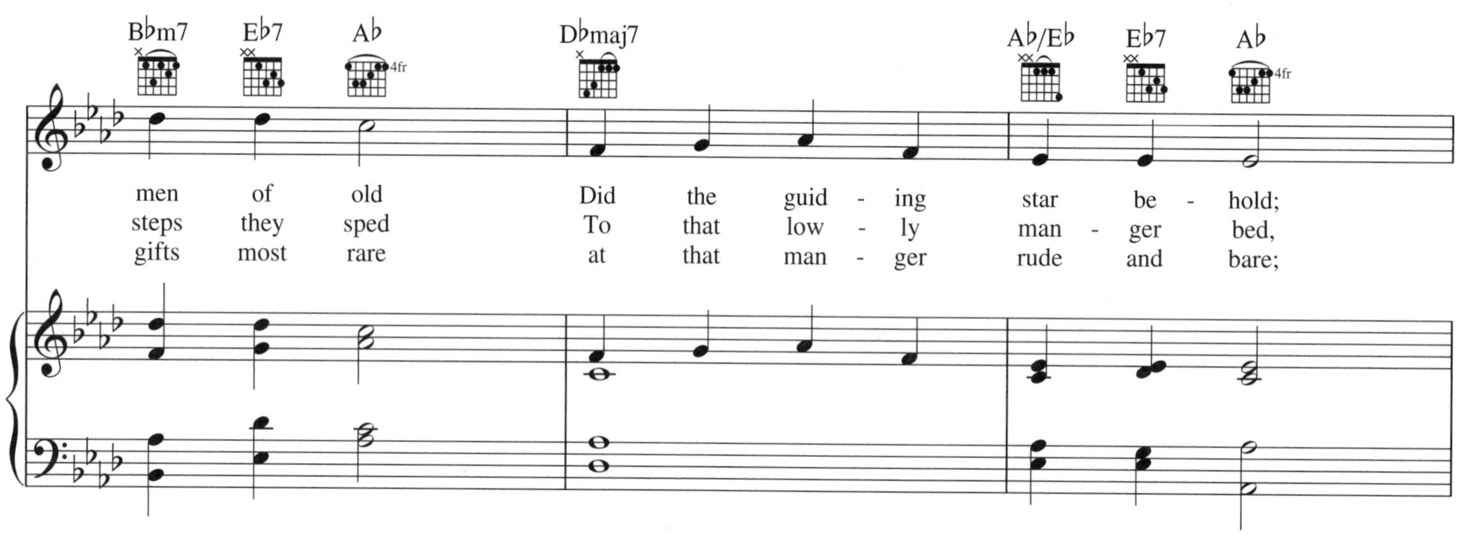


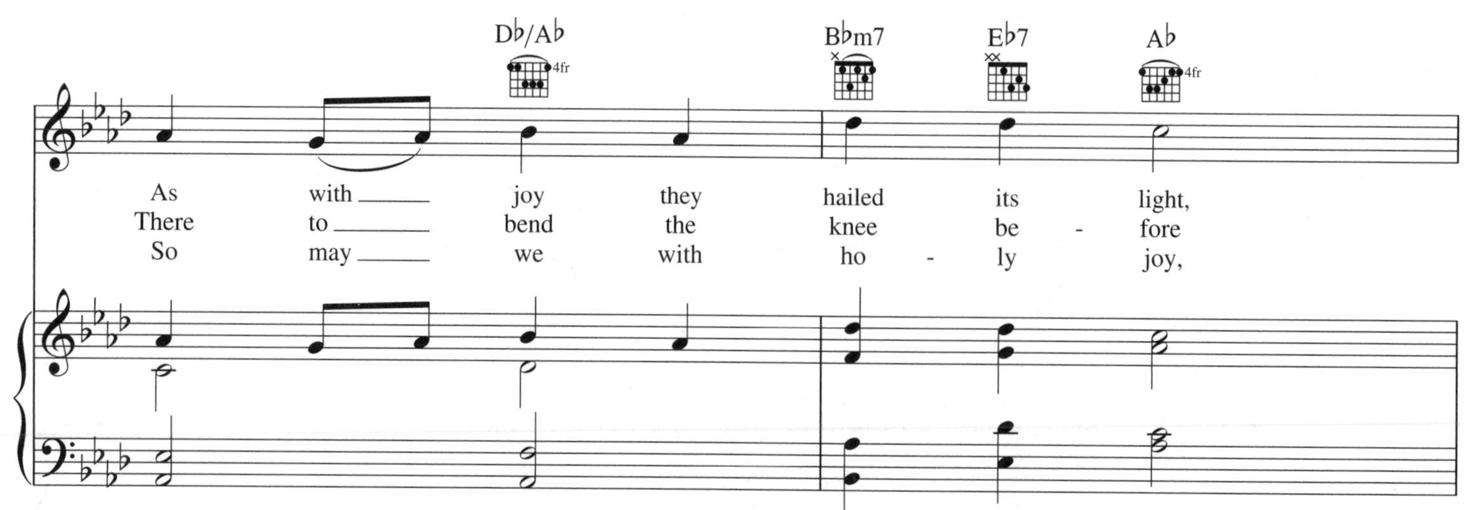

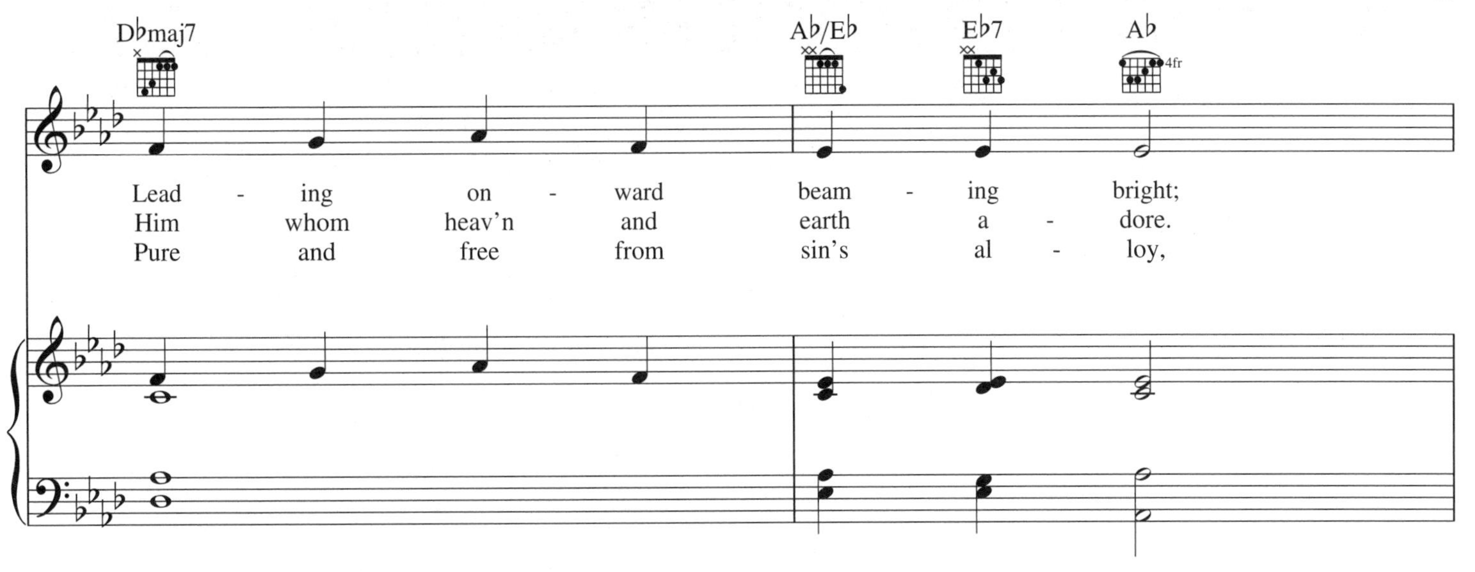

D♭maj7
A♭/E♭
E♭7
A♭
4fr
Lead - ing on - ward beam - ing bright;
Him whom heav'n and earth a - dore.
Pure and free from sin's al - loy,


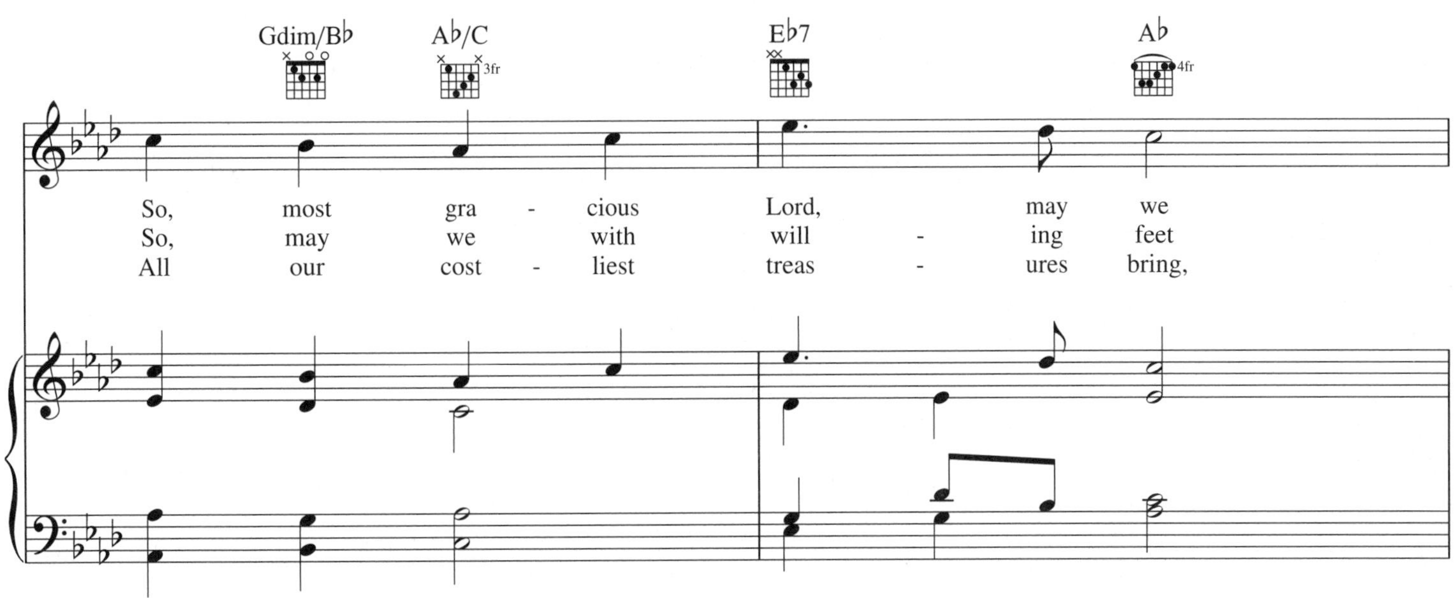

Gdim/B♭
A♭/C
3fr
E♭7
A♭
4fr
So, most gra - cious Lord, may we
So, may we with will - ing feet
All our cost - liest treas - ures bring,

D♭
Cm7
3fr
B♭m7
A♭/E♭
E♭7
A♭
4fr
Ev - er - more be led to Thee.
Ev - er seek Thy mer - cy seat.
Christ, to Thee, our heav'n - ly King.

# AT THE GATES OF HEAVEN ABOVE

Traditional Romanian Carol

# A BABE IS BORN IN BETHLEHEM

Translated by PHILIP SCHAFF
Music by LUDVIG LINDEMAN

# AULD LANG SYNE

Words by ROBERT BURNS
Traditional Scottish Melody

F/A
F
Dm
Gm
3fr
Gm/C
A7/C♯
Dm
Gm7
C7
auld ac - quain - tance be for - got and days of auld lang
syne? For auld lang syne, my dear, for
C9
auld lang syne we'll take a cup of
F7
B♭
G♯dim7
kind - ness yet for auld lang syne.
B♭/F

# AWAY IN A MANGER

Traditional
Words by JOHN T. McFARLAND (v.3)
Music by WILLIAM J. KIRKPATRICK

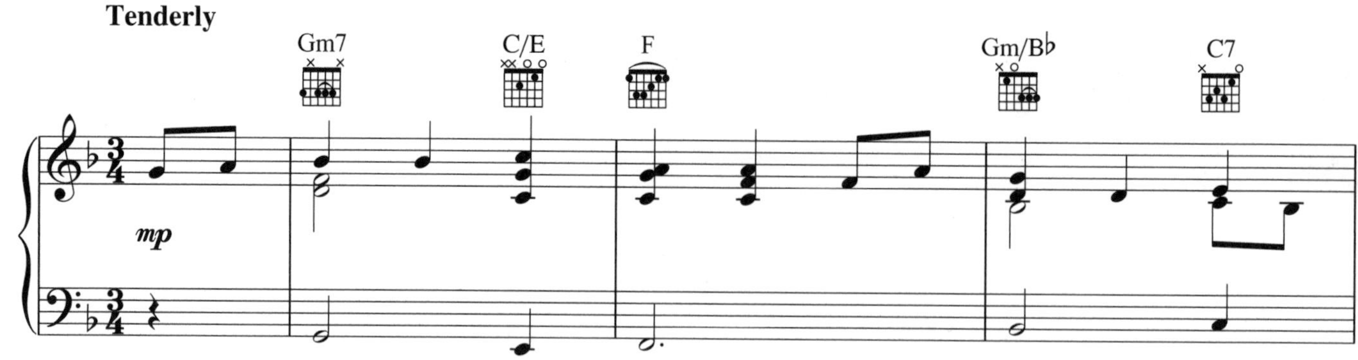


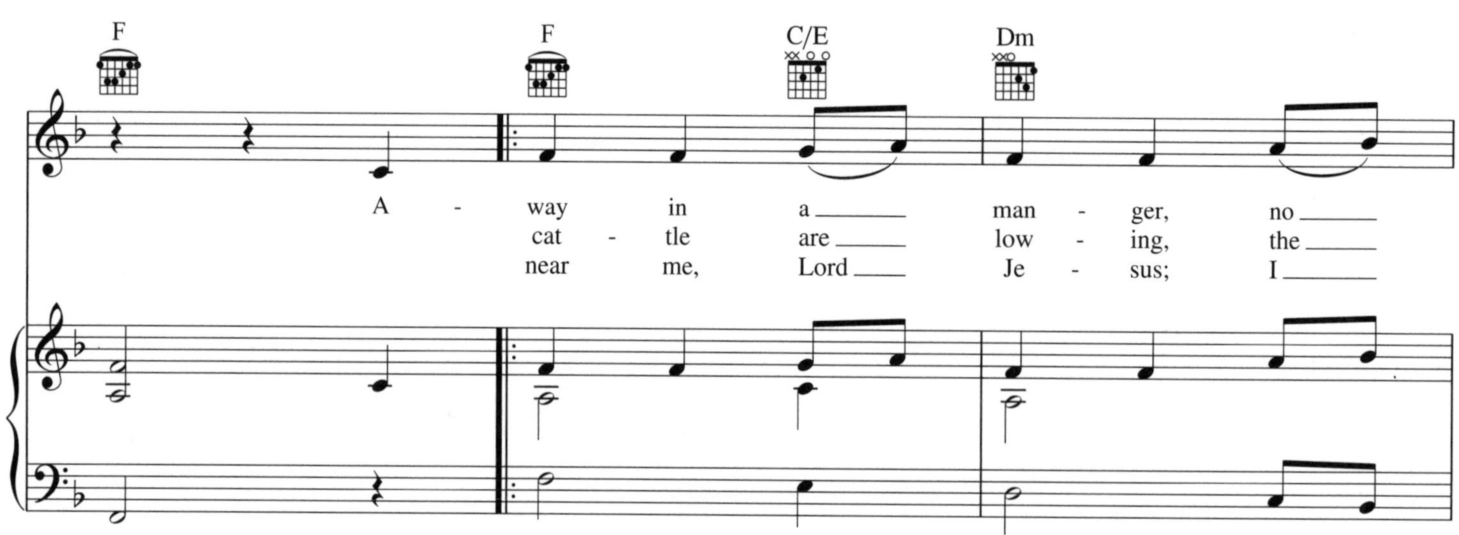


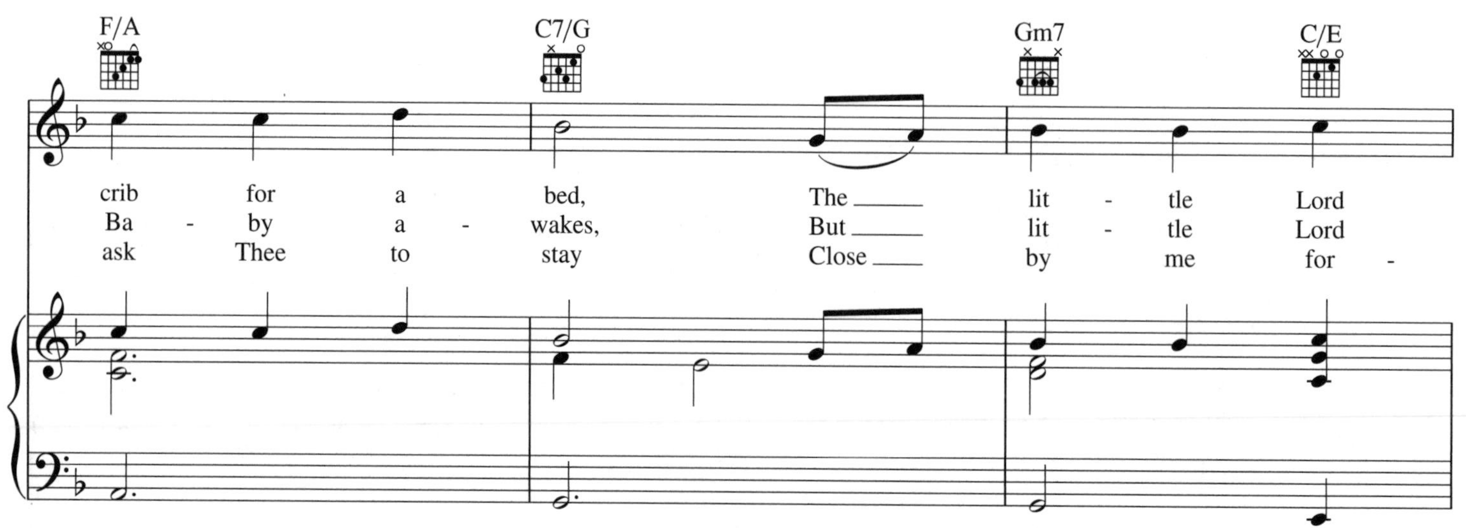

F
G/B
C
C7
Je - sus laid down His sweet head. The
Je - sus, no cry - ing He makes. I
ev - er and love me, I pray. Bless
F
C/E
Dm
F/A
stars in the bright sky looked down where He
love Thee, Lord Je - sus, look down from the
all the dear chil - dren in Thy ten - der
C7/G
Gm7
C/E
F
lay, The lit - tle Lord Je - sus a -
sky, And stay by my side un - til
care, And fit us for heav - en to
Gm/B♭
C7
1, 2
F
3
F
sleep on the hay. The
morn - ing is nigh. Be
live with Thee there.

# AWAY IN A MANGER

Traditional
Words by JOHN T. McFARLAND (v.3)
Music by JAMES R. MURRAY

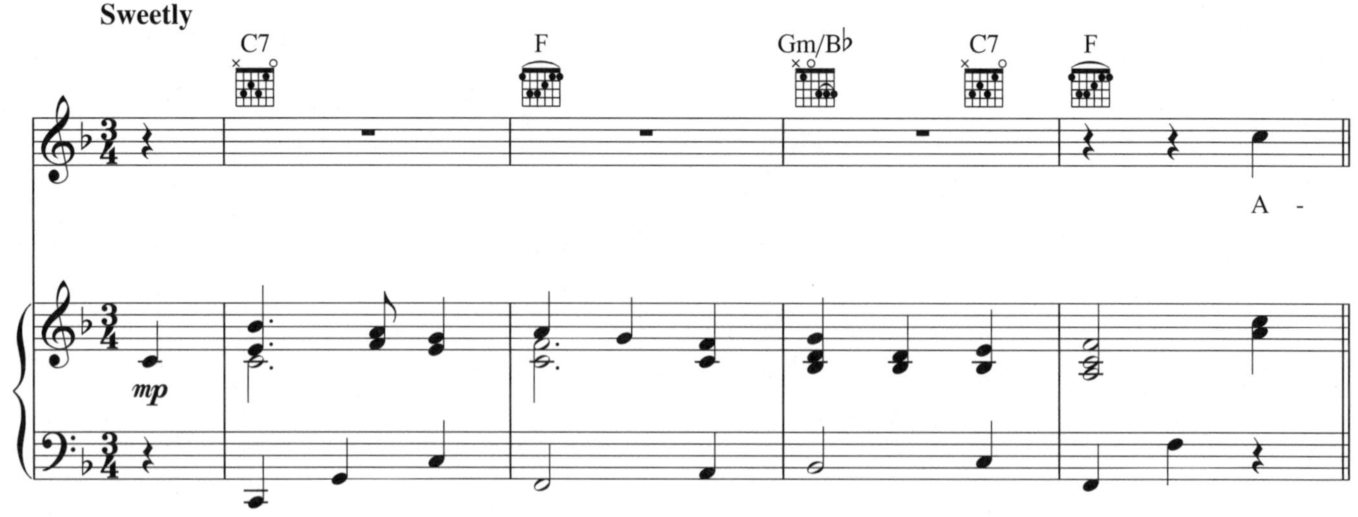

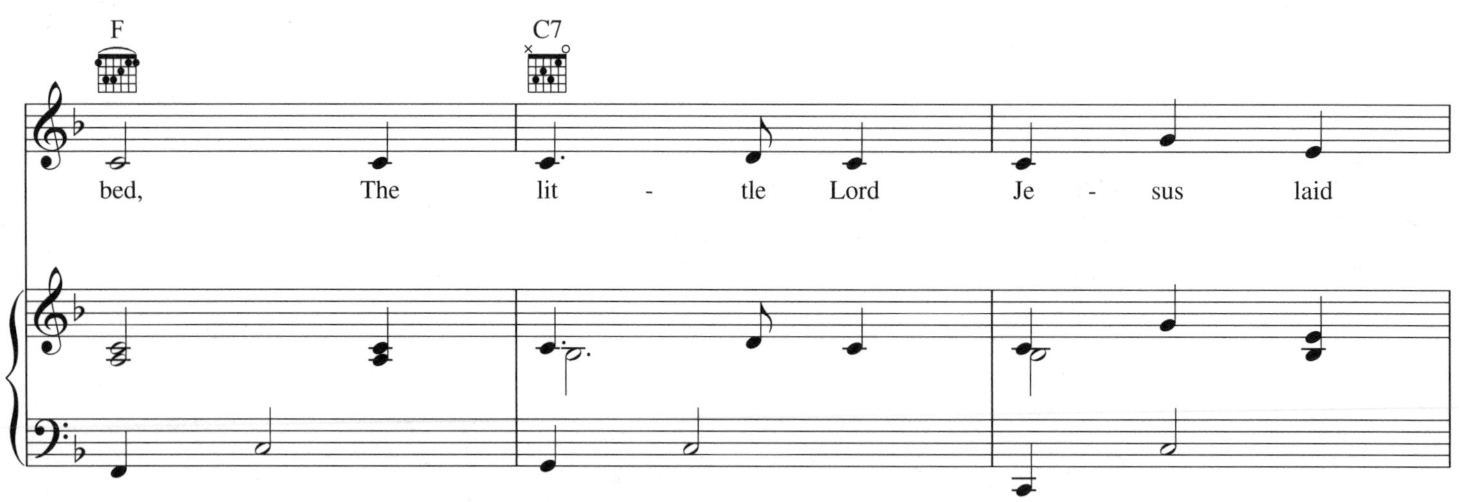

F
down His sweet head. The stars in the
B♭
F
sky looked down where He lay, The
C7
F
Gm/B♭
C7
F
lit - tle Lord Je - sus, a - sleep on the hay. The
B♭
cat - tle are low - ing, the ba - by a -

F
C7
wakes, But lit - tle Lord Je - sus, no
F
cry - ing He makes. I love Thee, Lord
B♭
F
Je - sus, look down from the sky, And
C7
F
Gm7
F/A
B♭
C7
F
stay by my cra - dle till morn - ing is nigh.

# BELLS OVER BETHLEHEM

Traditional Andalusian Carol

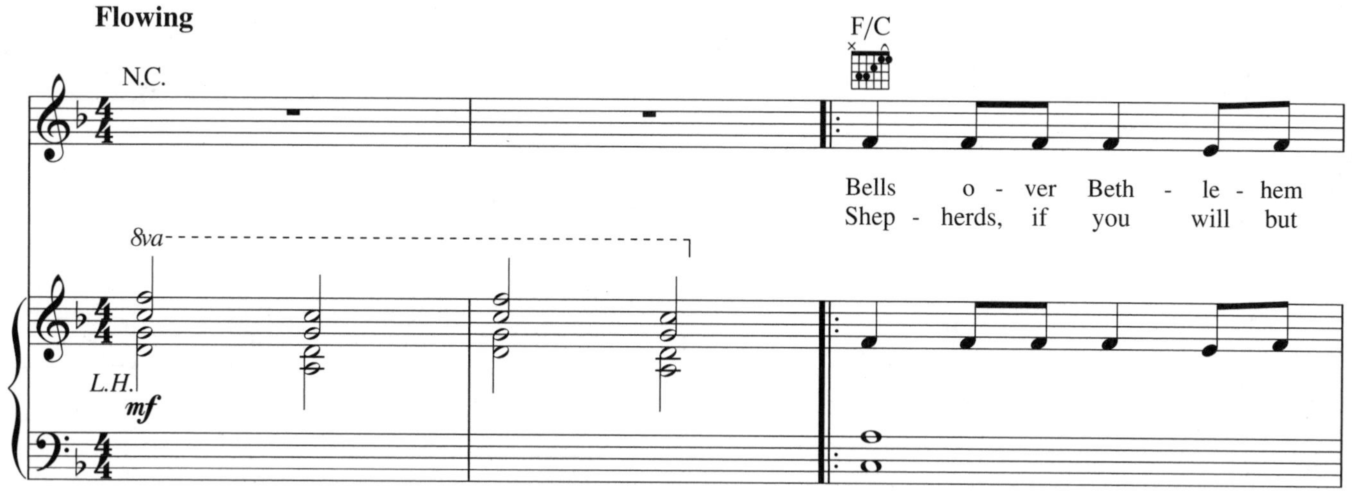


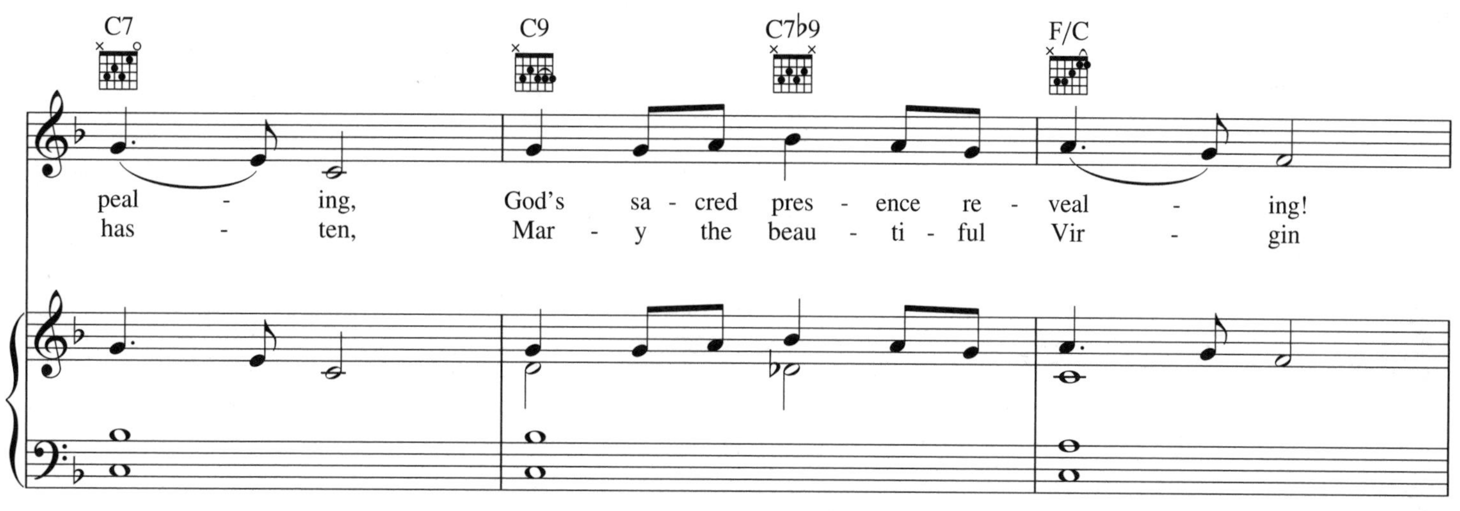


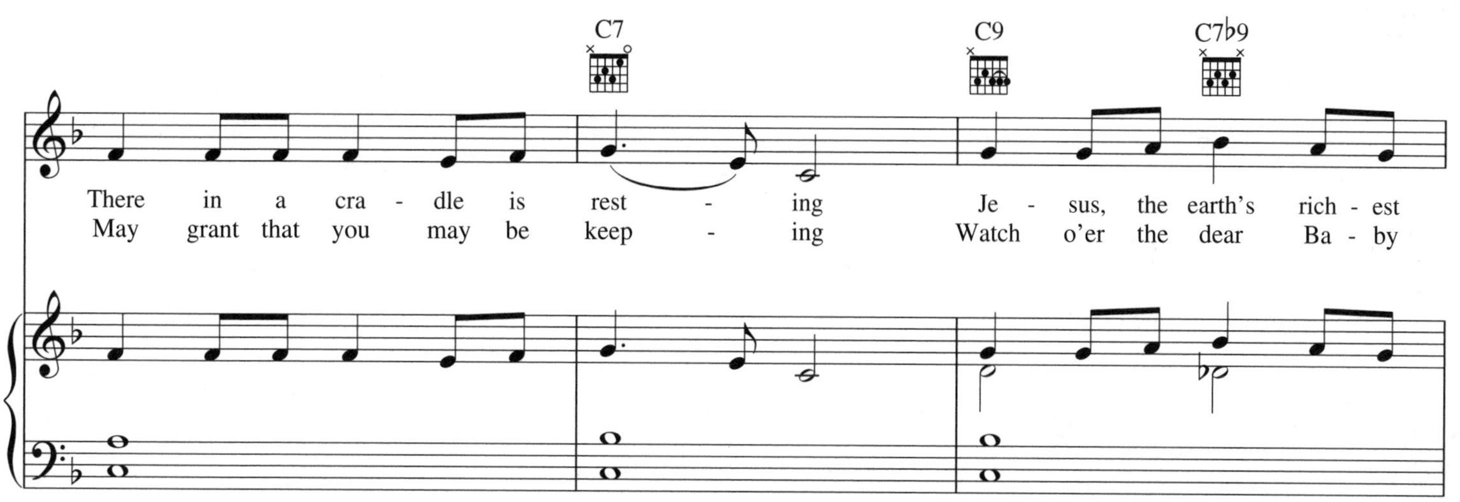

F/C
F
B♭/F
bless - ing!
sleep - ing.
The bells, the bells of Beth - le -
F
Em7♭5
Dm7
F/C
Fmaj7
C7
hem Are ring - ing out the tid - ings, "Good - will to all
F
B♭/F
F
Em7♭5
men!" Leave your sheep and come, O shep - herds,
8va
L.H.
Dm7
G7
Cdim7
F
C7
pres - ents bring the Babe so low - ly.

F
B♭/F
F
Em7♭5
Dm7
G7
Bring some cheese and bring some wine
For the moth - er
Cdim7
F
B♭/F
Mar - y ho - ly. The bells, the bells of Beth - le -
F
Em7♭5
Dm7
F/C
F/A
C7
hem Are ring - ing out the tid - ings, "Good - will to all
F
N.C.
men!"
8va
L.H.
rit.

# THE BABE

Traditional Mexican Lullaby Carol

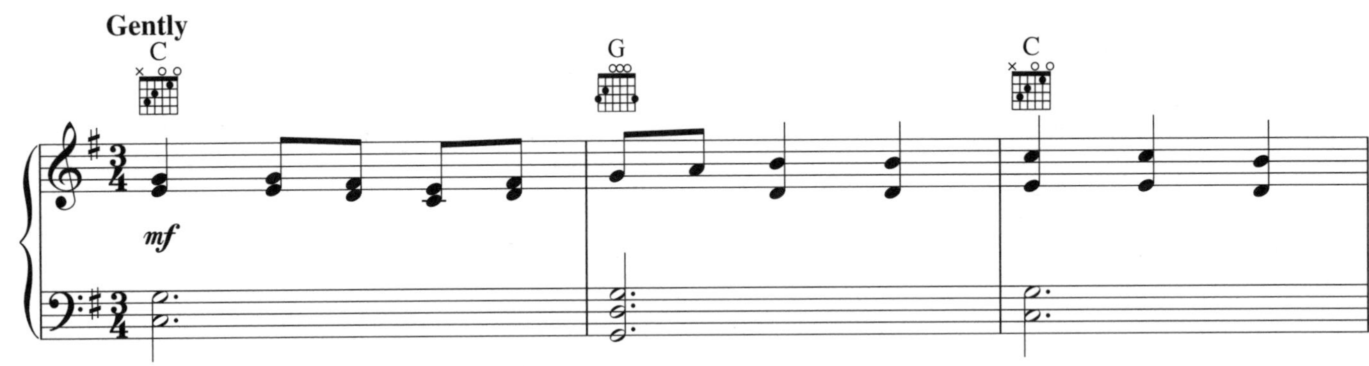


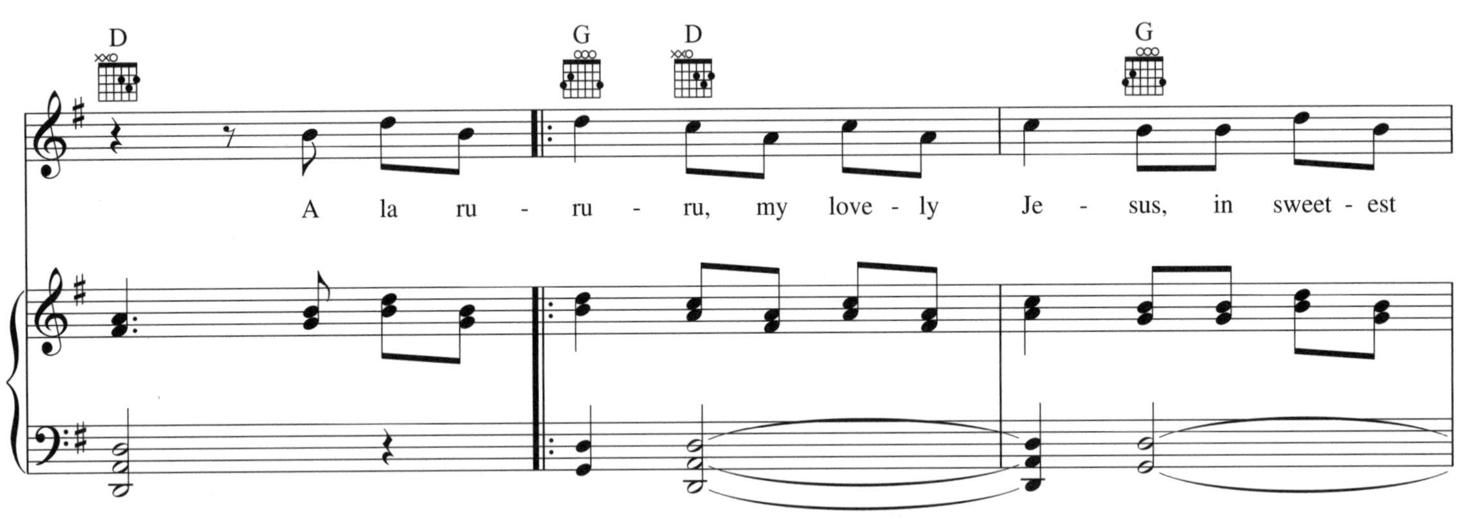


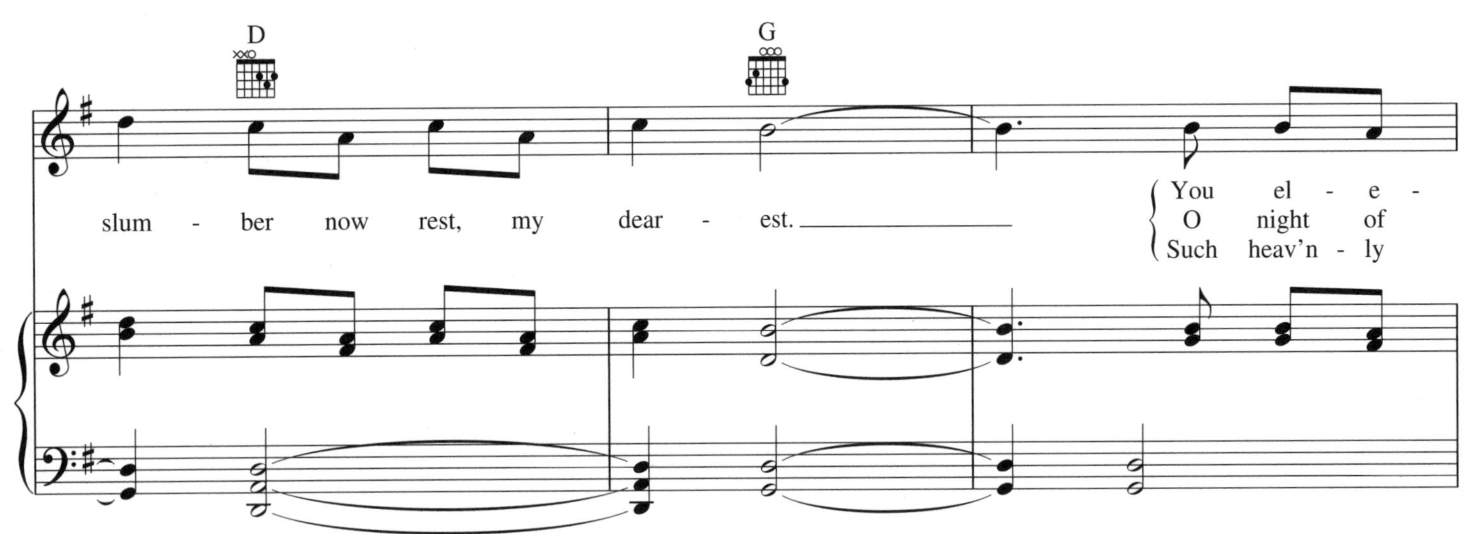

C
G
phant so huge, you small mos - qui - to, be ver - y
glo - ry, night of cel - e - bra - tion, so rich - ly
voic - es in sweet ac - cents sing - ing, the glo - rious
C
1, 2
B
3
B
still, you must not wake the Ba - by. A la ru -
blest by Mar - y, Queen of Heav - en. A la ru -
tid - ings of His birth are ring - ing! A la ru -
G
D
G
D
ru - ru, my love - ly Je - sus, in sweet - est slum - ber now rest, my
G
dear - est.

# A BABY IN THE CRADLE

By D.G. CORNER

G
G/B
Am/C
G/D
shin - eth as a mir - ror Re -
brings us peace and broth - er - hood If
serve with joy and heart - i - ness, Be
Thy great love o'er - flow - ing Come
Am/C
D7
G7
G7/B
C
flects a no - ble light. This ti - ny
we but heed His Word, Doth Je - sus
hum - ble and be kind, For Mar - y's
flood - ing through my soul, Thou love - ly
D7
1-3
G
4
G
Child so bright. The
Christ, the Lord. And
Child so fine. O
Babe so small.
rit.

# BESIDE THY CRADLE HERE I STAND

Words by PAUL GERHARDT
Translated by REV. J. TROUTBECK
Music from the *Geistliche Gesangbuch*

D7
G
C
G/B
will - ing hand The ver - y gifts Thou
Am7
D7
G
F♯m7♭5
4fr
B7
giv - est. Ac - cept me, 'tis my
Em7
A7
D7
G
G/B
mind and heart, My soul, my strength, my
C6
B7
E7
E♭7
G/D
Am/C
G/B
C6
D7
G
ev - 'ry part That Thou from me re - quir - est.

# THE BIRTHDAY OF A KING

Words and Music by
WILLIAM H. NEIDLINGER

A♭6
B♭7
E♭7
B♭m7
E♭7/B♭
3fr
6fr
place where Je - sus lay.
per - fect ho - ly way.
Al - le - lu - ia, O how the
A♭
4fr
Fm7
B♭7
E♭7
an - gels sang! Al - le - lu - ia, how it rang! And the
C7
Fm
Dm7♭5
E♭7
A♭
B♭9
A♭/E♭
E♭7
sky was bright with a ho - ly light; 'twas the birth - day of a
A♭
E♭/G
D♭/F
D♭m/F♭
1
E♭7sus
E♭7
A♭
2
E♭7sus
E♭7
A♭
King!
'Twas a

# THE BOAR'S HEAD CAROL

Traditional English

G C Em F Dm7 G C
Ca - put a - pri de - fe - ro, Res - dens lau - des Do - mi - no. The
G C G/B C F G C
boar's head I un - der - stand, The fin - est dish in all the land. Which is
G C G/B C F G C
thus all be-decked with gay gar - land, Let us ser - vi - re can - ti - co,
G C Em F Dm7 G C
Ca - put a - pri de - fe - ro, Re - dens lau - des Do - mi - no.

# BRING A TORCH, JEANNETTE, ISABELLA

17th Century French Provençal Carol

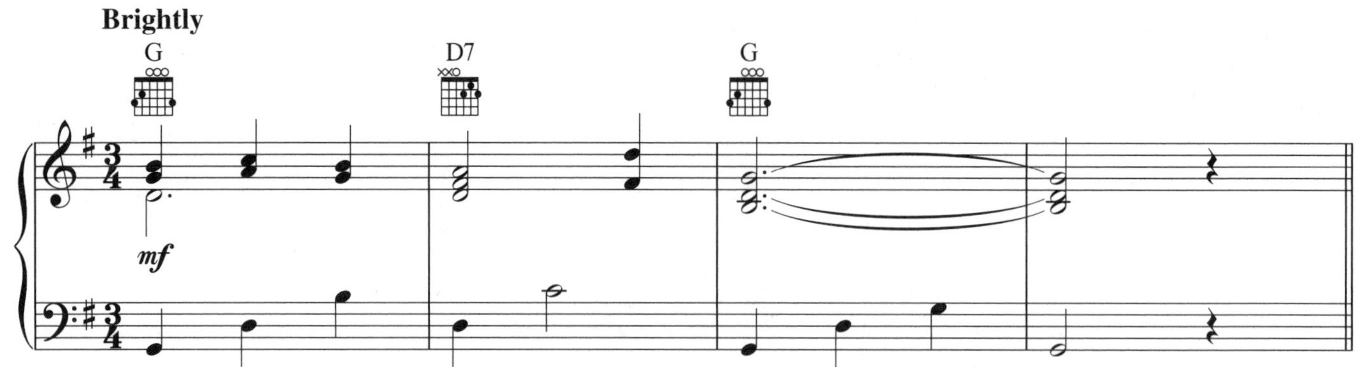


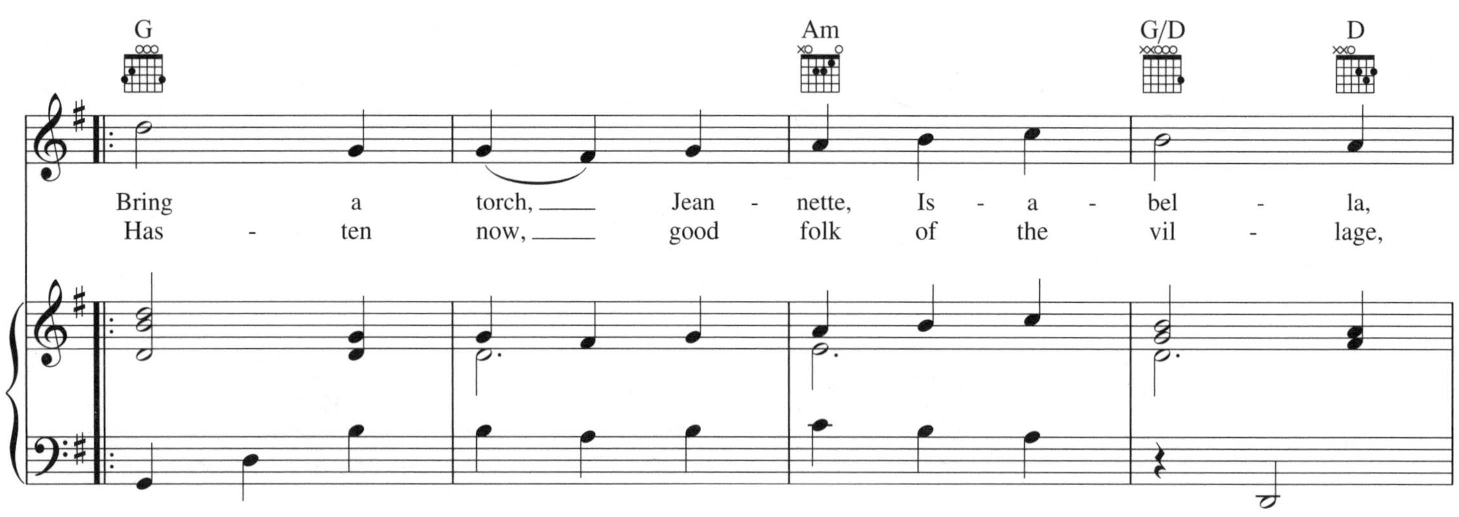


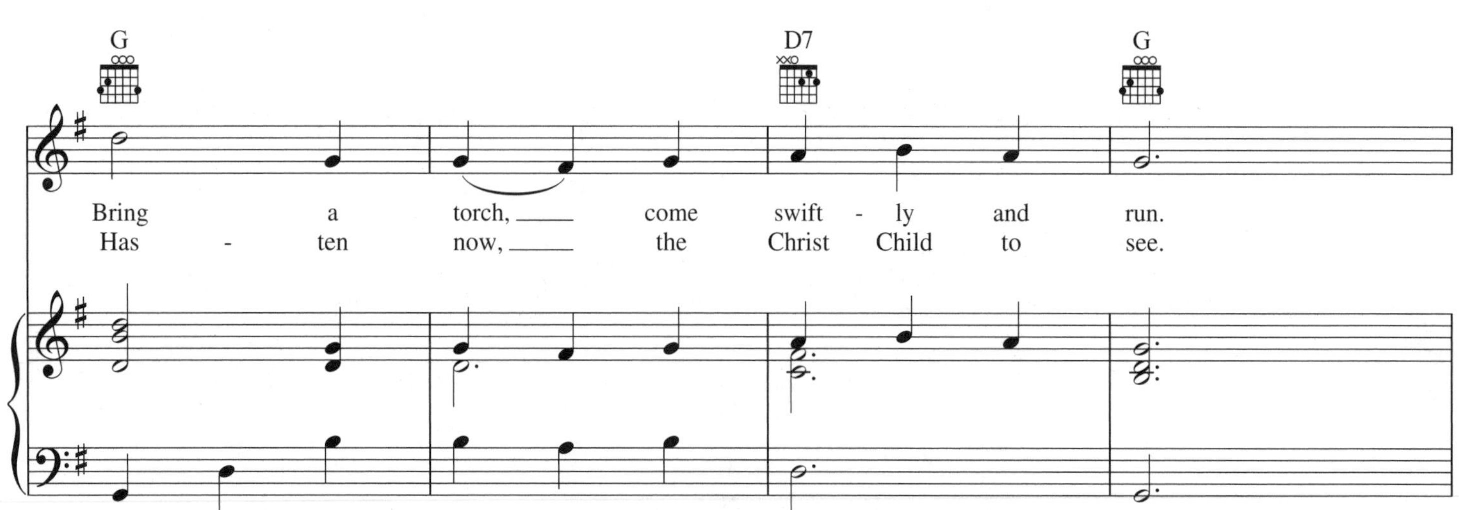

G/D
D
Christ is born; tell the folk of the vil - lage.
You will find Him a - sleep in a man - ger.
C
G/B
D7/A
G
D7
Em
Je - sus is sleep - ing in His cra - dle. Ah,
Qui - et - ly come and whis - per soft - ly. Hush,
D
G
D7
G
D7
Em
ah, Beau - ti - ful is the Moth - er. Ah,
hush, Peace - ful - ly now He slum - bers. Hush,
D
G
D7
G
ah, Beau - ti - ful is her Son.
hush, Peace - ful - ly now He sleeps.

# CAROL OF THE BAGPIPERS

Traditional Sicilian Carol

F
C7
bright as noon, a star. Nev - er so bright - ly nev - er so
F
C7
F
white - ly, shone the stars, as on that night! The
C
bright - est star went a - way to call the
F
C
F
Wise Men from the O - ri - ent.

# CAROL OF THE BIRDS

Traditional Catalonian Carol

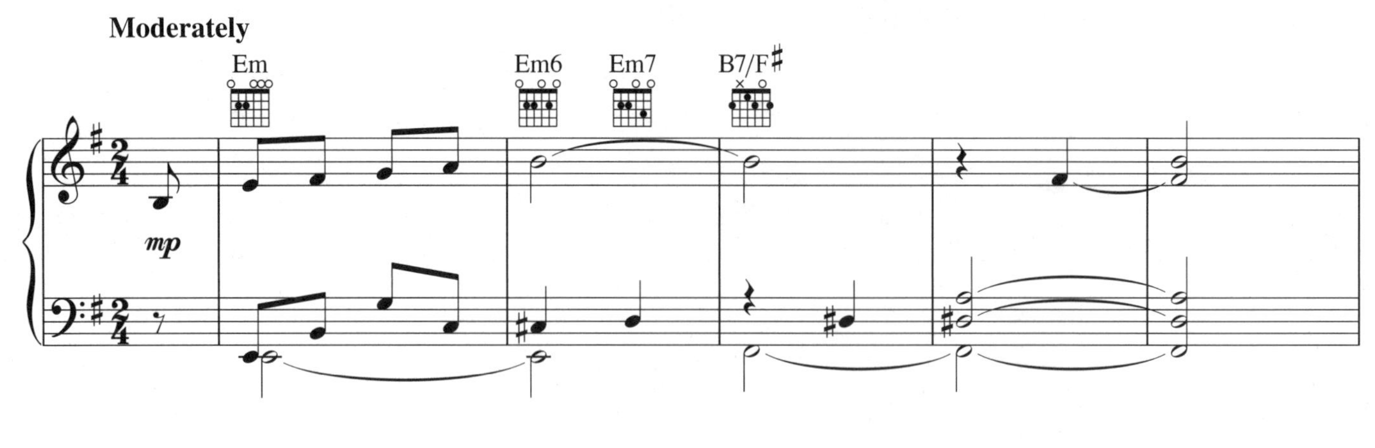


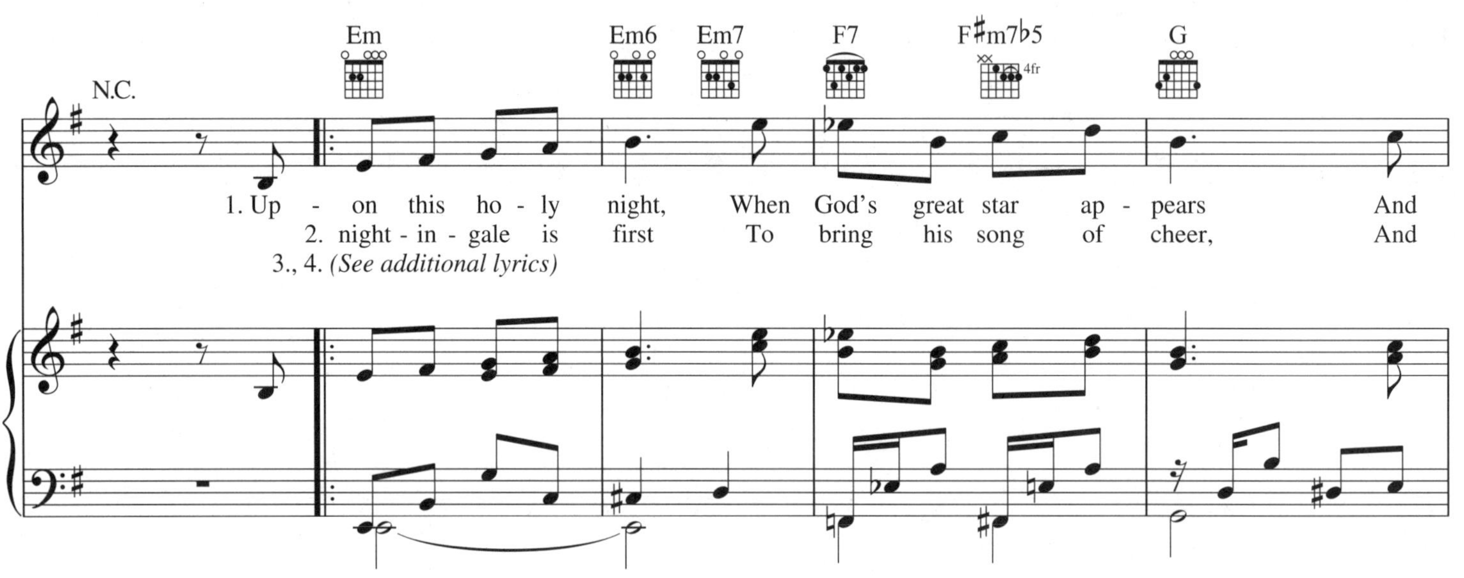


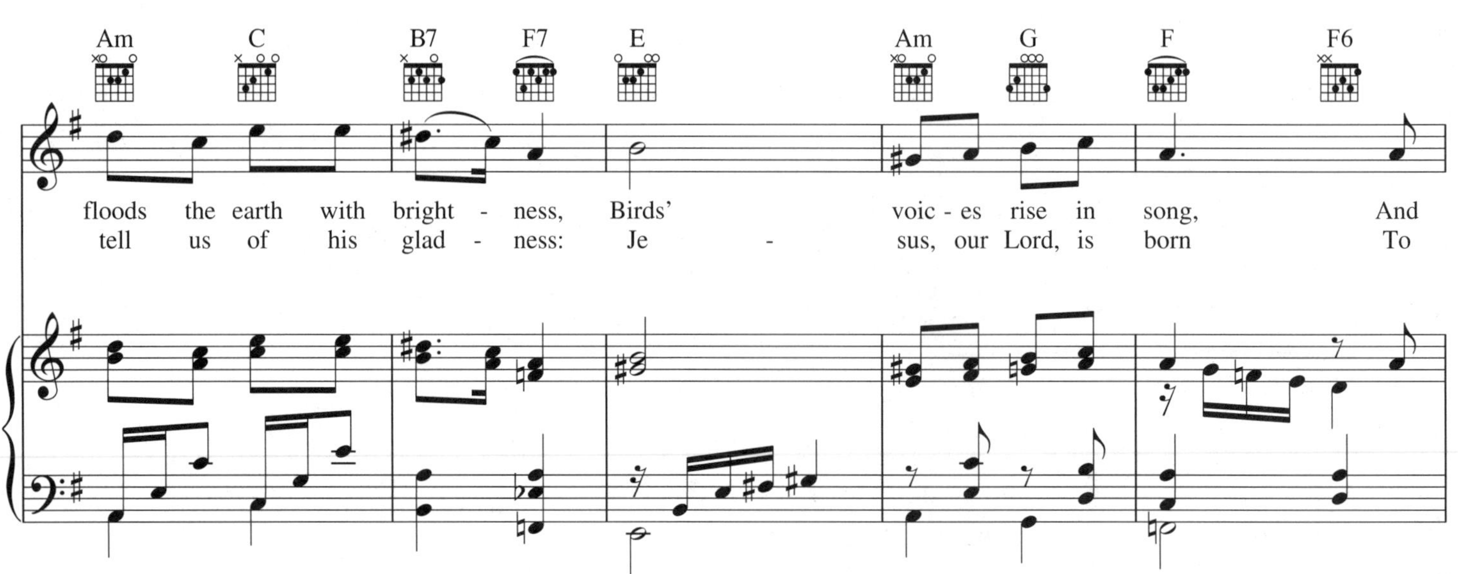

*Additional Lyrics*

3. The answ'ring Sparrow cries:
"God comes to earth this day
Amid the angels flying."
Trilling in sweetest tones,
The Finch his Lord now owns:
"To Him be all thanksgiving."
Trilling in sweetest tones,
The Finch his Lord now owns:
"To Him be all thanksgiving."

4. The Partridge adds his note:
"To Bethlehem I'll fly,
Where in the stall He's lying.
There, near the manger blest,
I'll build myself a nest,
And sing my love undying.
There, near the manger blest,
I'll build myself a nest,
And sing my love undying."

# THE CHERRY TREE CAROL

Traditional English Carol

# A CHILD IS BORN IN BETHLEHEM

14th-Century Latin Text adapted by
NICOLAI F.S. GRUNDTVIG
Traditional Danish Melody

# CHILD JESUS

Words by HANS CHRISTIAN ANDERSEN
Music by NIELS GADE

B♭
Cm
Gm
D
Gm
B♭7
'round Him no light shone. But
heav'n - ly bliss can gain. Let
E♭
B♭
C/E
Fm
B♭
E♭
A♭
Fm
Heav - en sent a star so bright, and ox - en kissed His
us, with child - like heart and mind, seek now the Son of
G
Cm
A♭
B♭
Cm
D
Gm
Cm
feet that night.
God to find.
Al - le - lu - ia, Al - le - lu - ia, Al -
A♭
B♭7
1
E♭
2
E♭
le - lu - ia! O ia!
3fr
4fr

# CHRIST IS BORN THIS EVENING

Traditional

G7
C
G7
C
dawn - ing! An - gels from on high are sing - ing
low - ly. See, the star on high is gleam - ing,
G7
C
To the One who comes from Heav - en:
O'er the love - ly In - fant beam - ing!
F
E
Glo - ri - a, glo - ri - a, glo - ri - a,
Am
G/B
F/C
G7/D
C/G
G7
C
In ex - cel - sis De - o!

# CHRIST WAS BORN ON CHRISTMAS DAY

Traditional

**Lilting**

F/C Bb/D F/C C7 F

*mf*

F

Christ was born on Christ - mas day,

Wreath the hol - ly, twine the bay;

Gm C7 F C/E F/C Bb/D

*Chris - tus na - tus ho - di - e;* The Babe, the Son, the

F/C
C7
F
Ho - ly One of Mar - y.
Christ was born on Christ - mas day, Wreath the hol - ly,
twine the bay;
C7
Chris - tus na - tus ho - di - e; The
F
B♭
F/C
C7
F
Babe, the Son, the Ho - ly One of Mar - y.

# CHRISTIANS, AWAKE! SALUTE THE HAPPY MORN

Words by JOHN BYROM
Music by JOHN WAINWRIGHT

G7
E7
F
F♯dim7
love which hosts of an - gels chant - ed
birth to you and all the na - tions
C/G
G♯dim
3fr
Am
F
G7
G♯dim7
from a - bove. With them the
up - on earth: This day hath
Am7
D7
Dm
Em
F6
F♯dim
9fr
G7
joy - ful tid - ings first be - gun of
God ful - filled His prom - ised Word; this
F
G7
C
G7/B
Am7
Fm/A♭
C/G
G7
C
God in - car - nate and the Vir - gin's Son.
day is born a Sav - ior, Christ the Lord."

# COVENTRY CAROL

Words by ROBERT CROO
Traditional English Melody

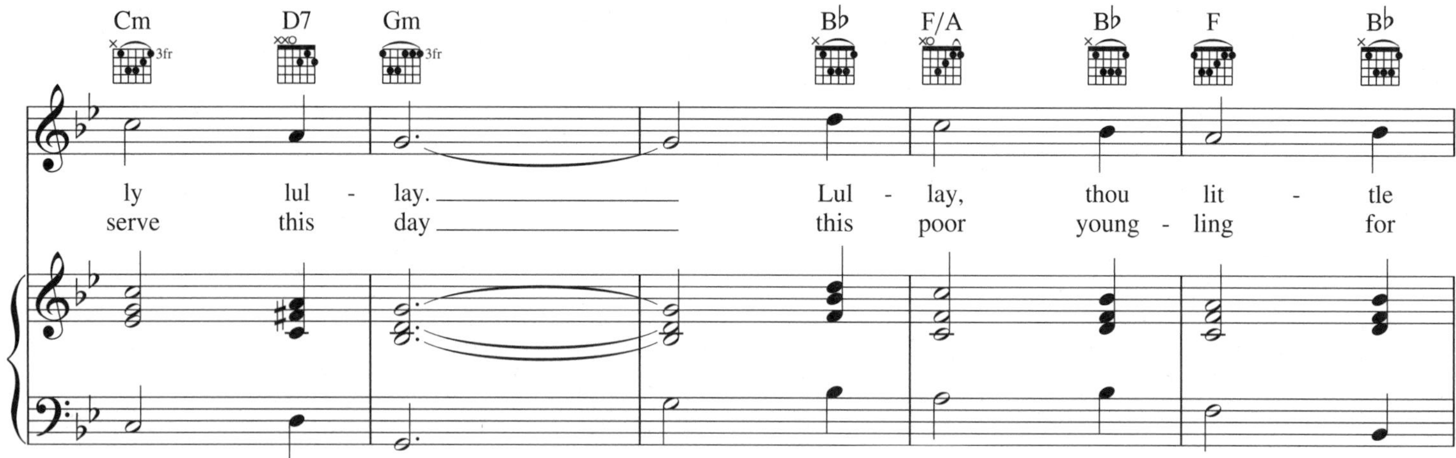


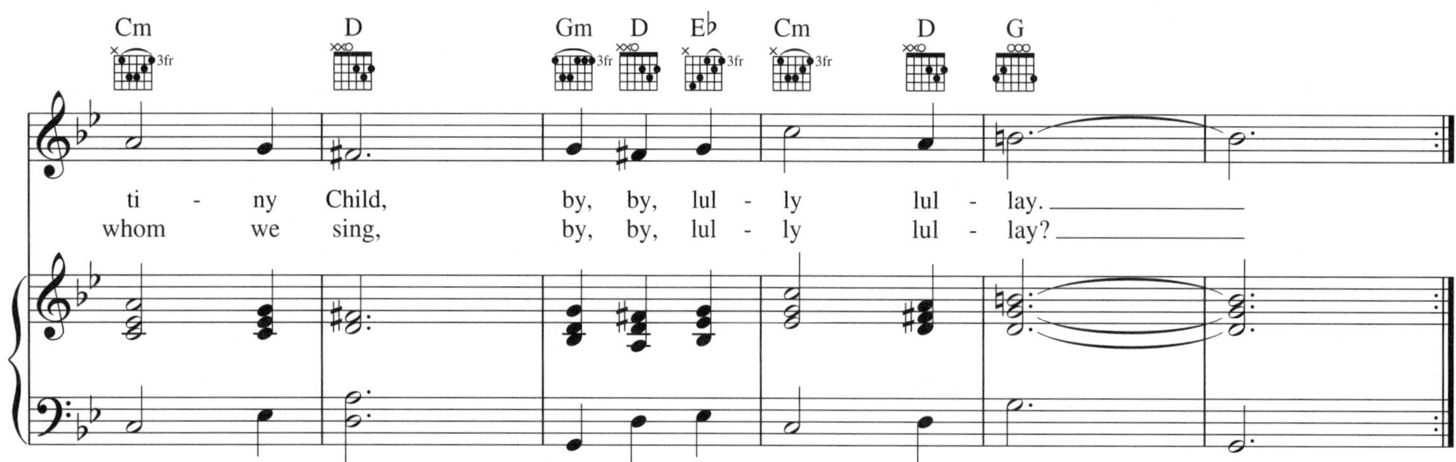


*Additional Lyrics*

3. Herod the king,
In his raging,
Charged he hath this day.
His men of might,
In his own sight,
All young children to slay.

4. That woe is me,
Poor child for thee!
And ever morn and day,
For thy parting
Neither say nor sing
By, by, lully lullay!

# GLAD CHRISTMAS BELLS

Traditional American Carol

*Additional Lyrics*

3. Nor raiment gay as there He lay,
Adorn'd the infant stranger;
Poor humble child of mother mild
She laid Him in a manger.

4. But from afar, a splendid star
The wise men westward turning;
The livelong night saw pure and bright,
Above His birthplace burning.

# A DAY, BRIGHT DAY OF GLORY

Traditional

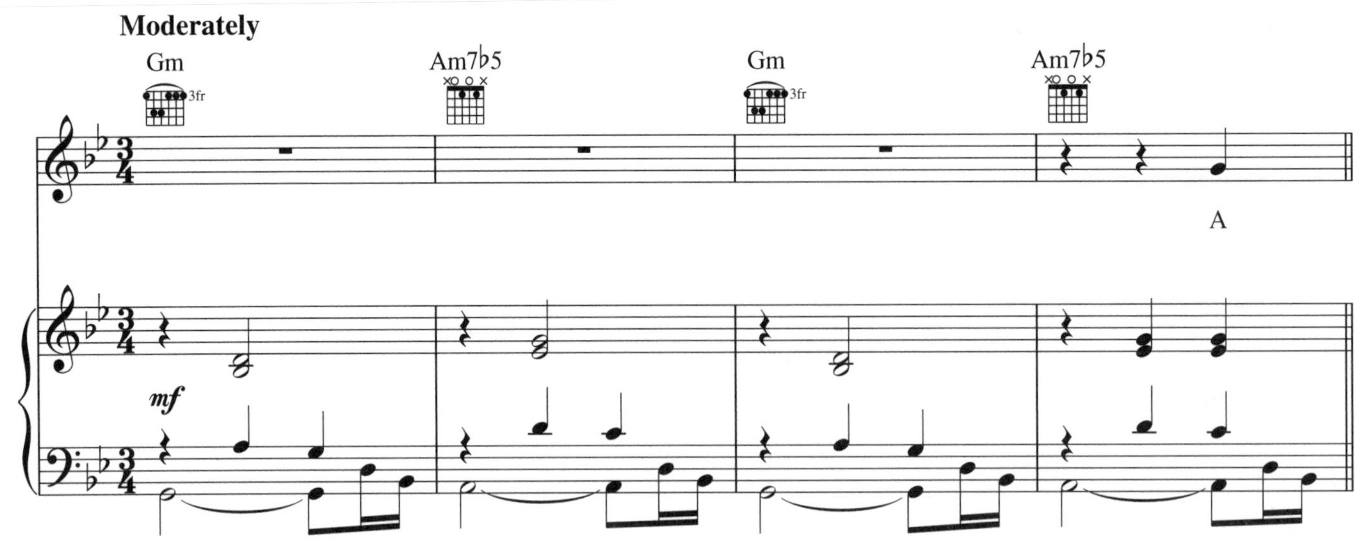

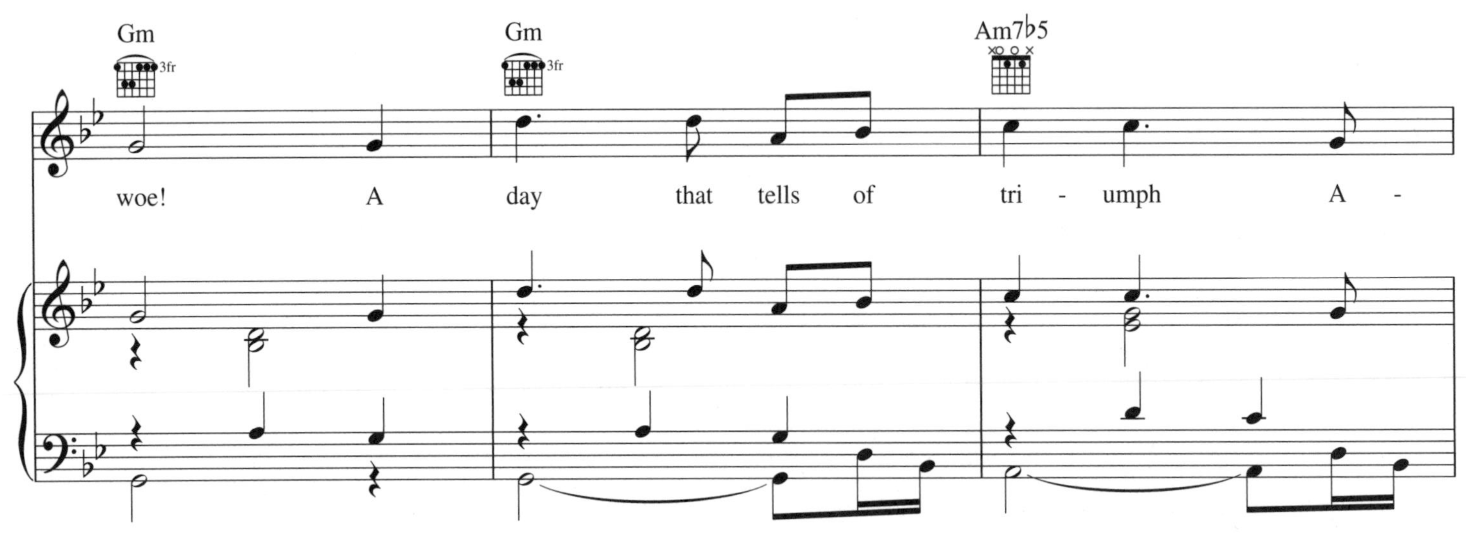

Eb9
D7b9
Gm
D7#9
Ebmaj7
gainst our van - quished foe! For us this Christ - mas
Cm7
Fsus2/A
Am7b5
D7
Eb7/Bb
sun - rise, this bright De - cem - ber morn, so
D7#9
Ebmaj7
Cm7
Fsus2/A
D7
sing, let us be joy - ous For Christ, our Lord is
Gm
Am7b5
D7#9
Gm(maj13)
born!

# DECK THE HALL

Traditional Welsh Carol

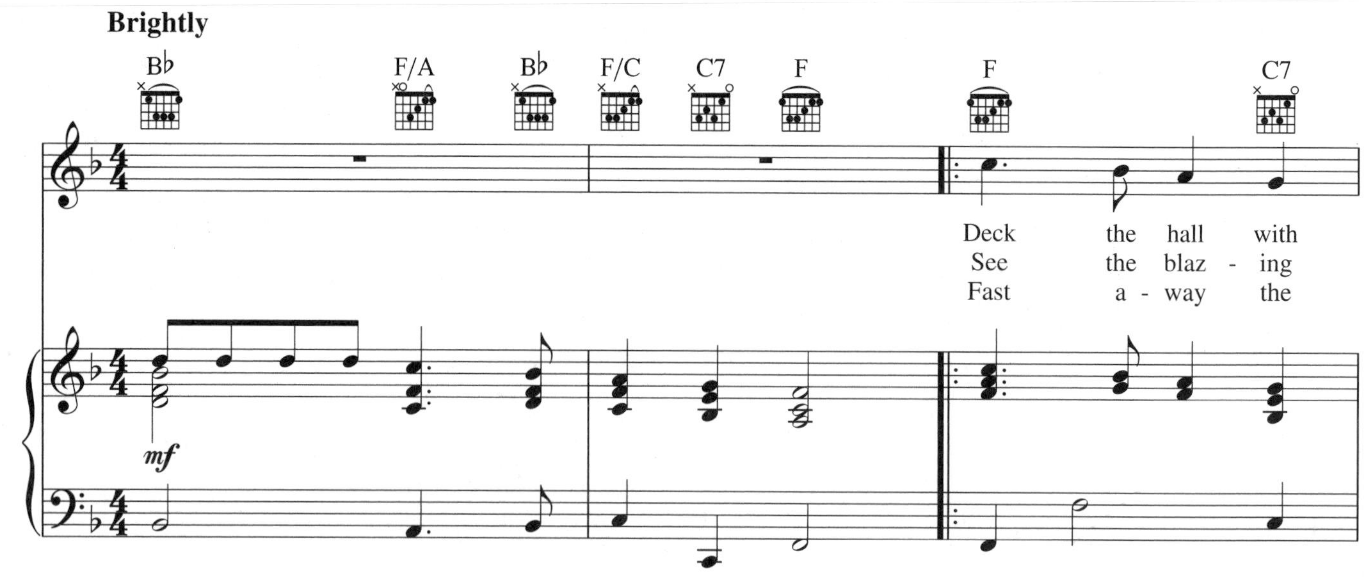

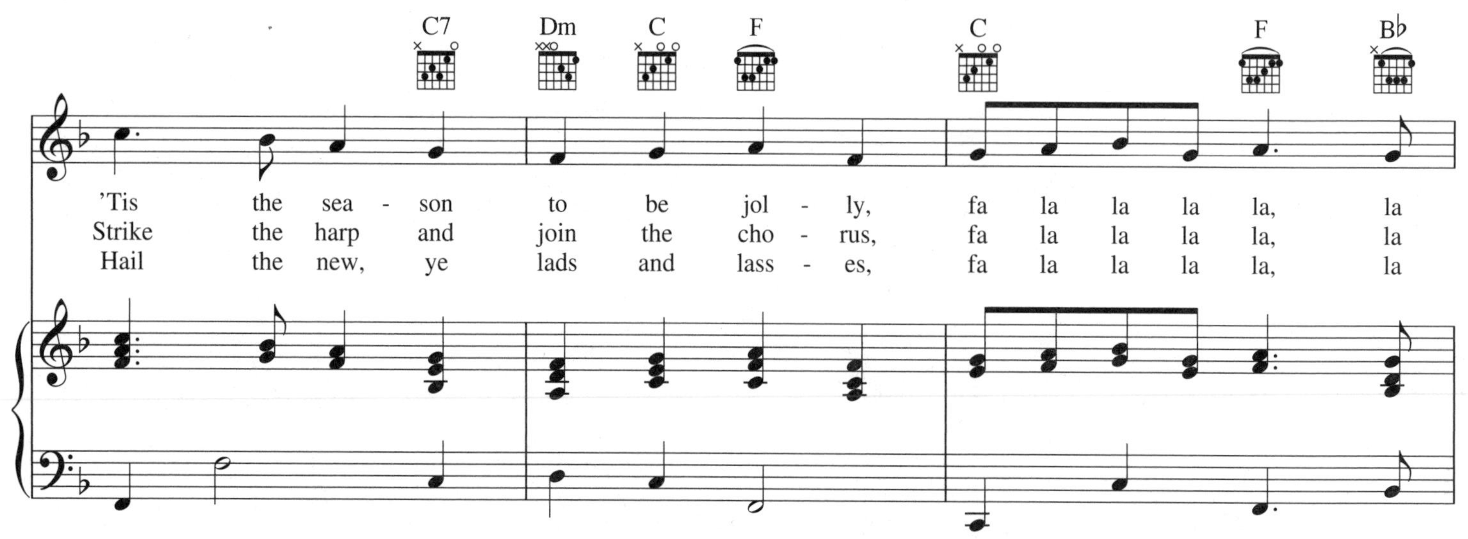

F/C
C
F
C
F
C
la la la. Don we now our gay ap - par - el,
la la la. Fol - low me in mer - ry meas - ure,
la la la. Sing we joy - ous all to - geth - er,

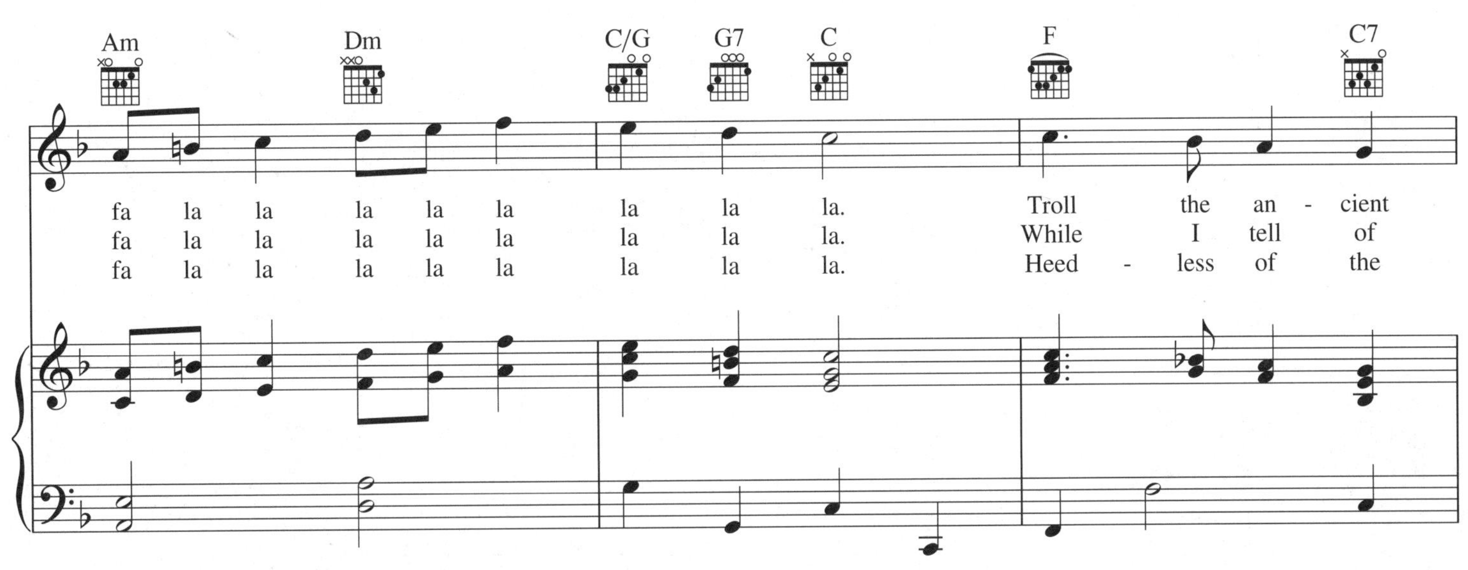
Am
Dm
C/G
G7
C
F
C7
fa la la la la la la la la. Troll the an - cient
fa la la la la la la la la. While I tell of
fa la la la la la la la la. Heed - less of the

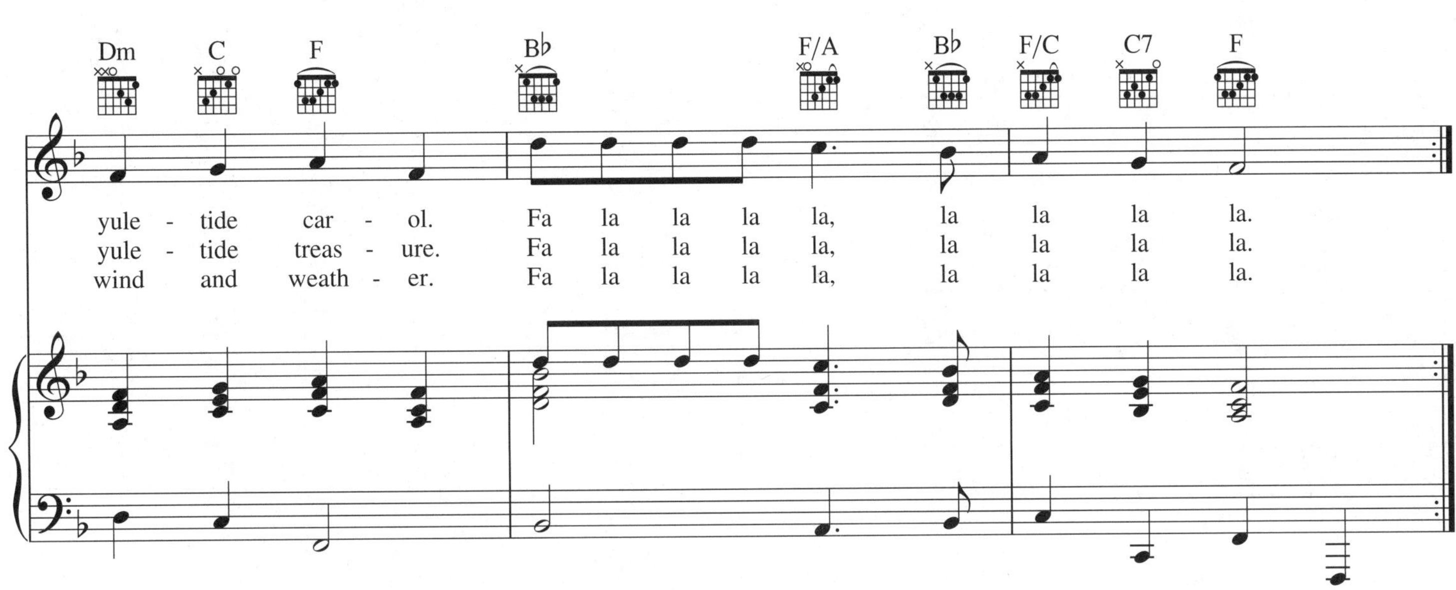
Dm
C
F
B♭
F/A
B♭
F/C
C7
F
yule - tide car - ol. Fa la la la la, la la la la.
yule - tide treas - ure. Fa la la la la, la la la la.
wind and weath - er. Fa la la la la, la la la la.

# DING DONG! MERRILY ON HIGH!

French Carol

B♭
Dm
Gm7
Cm7
F7
sing - ing.
sung - en.
sing - ers.
Glo - -
Dm
Gm
Am7♭5
D7
Gm
Cm7
- - -
F7
B♭/D
E♭
E♭maj7
C7/E
F7
B♭
- ri - a, Ho - san - na in ex - cel - sis!

# EVERYWHERE, EVERYWHERE, CHRISTMAS TONIGHT

By LEWIS H. REDNER
and PHILLIPS BROOKS

C G/D B7/D♯
Christ - mas where snow peaks stand sol - emn and
Christ - mas where peace like a dove in its
Em A7/C♯ G/D
white, Christ - mas where corn - fields lie
flight broods o'er brave men in the
D7 G/D D♯dim7 Em A7/C♯ G/D
sun - ny and bright. Ev - 'ry - where,
thick of the fight. Ev - 'ry - where,
C/E G/D C♯dim7 G/D D7 G
ev - 'ry - where, Christ - mas to - night.
ev - 'ry - where, Christ - mas to - night.

# THE FIRST NOËL

17th Century English Carol
Music from W. Sandys' *Christmas Carols*

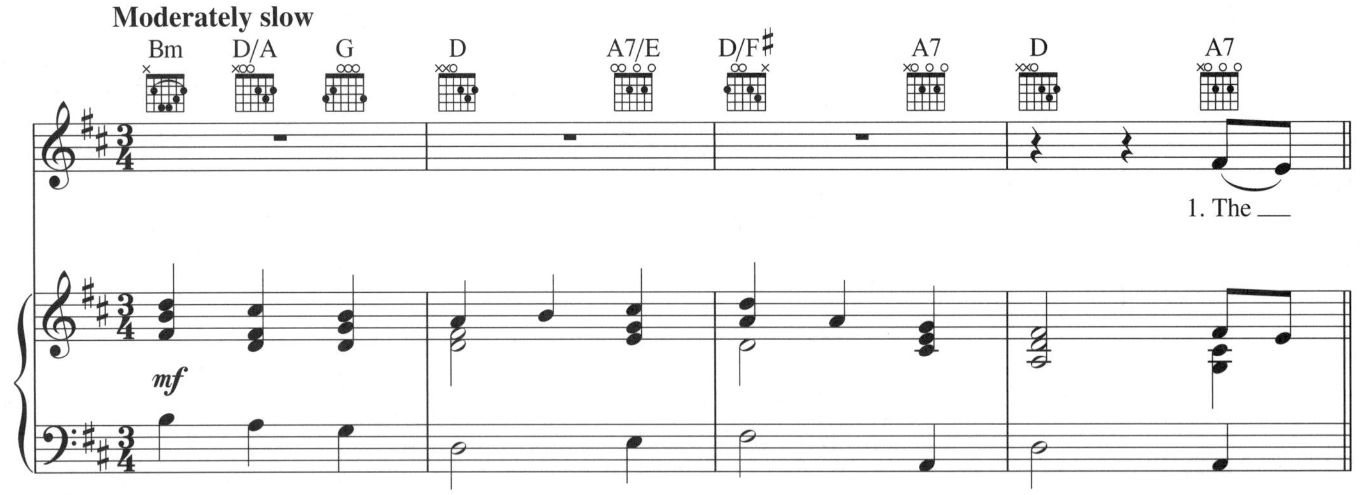


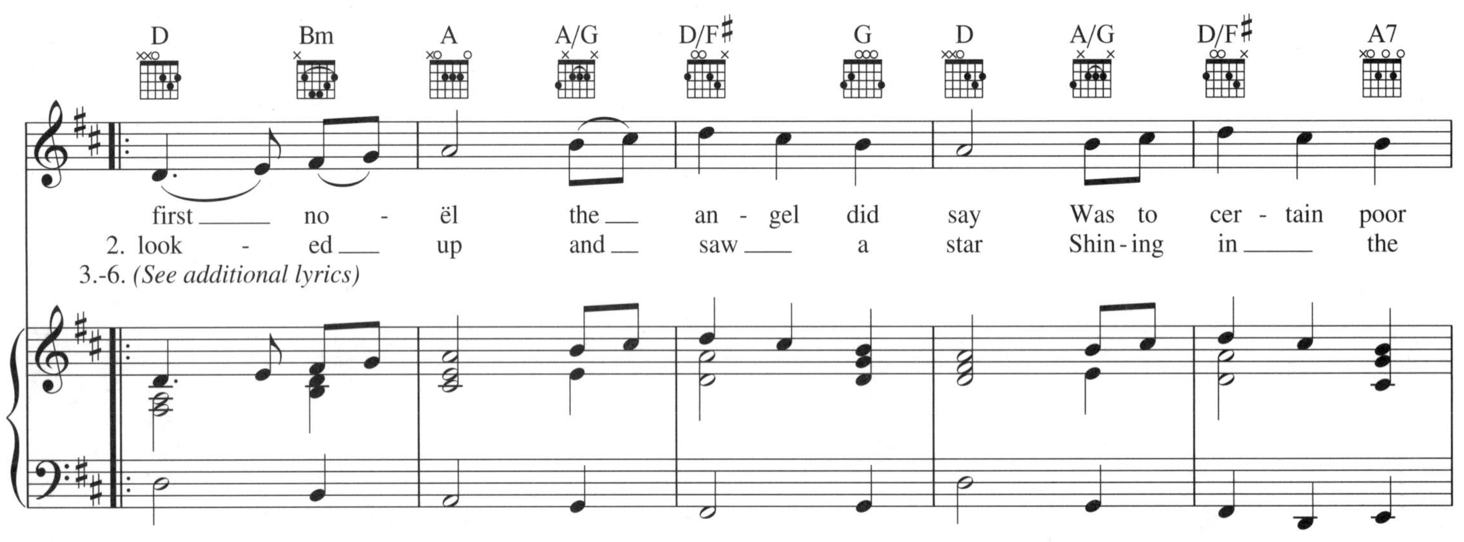


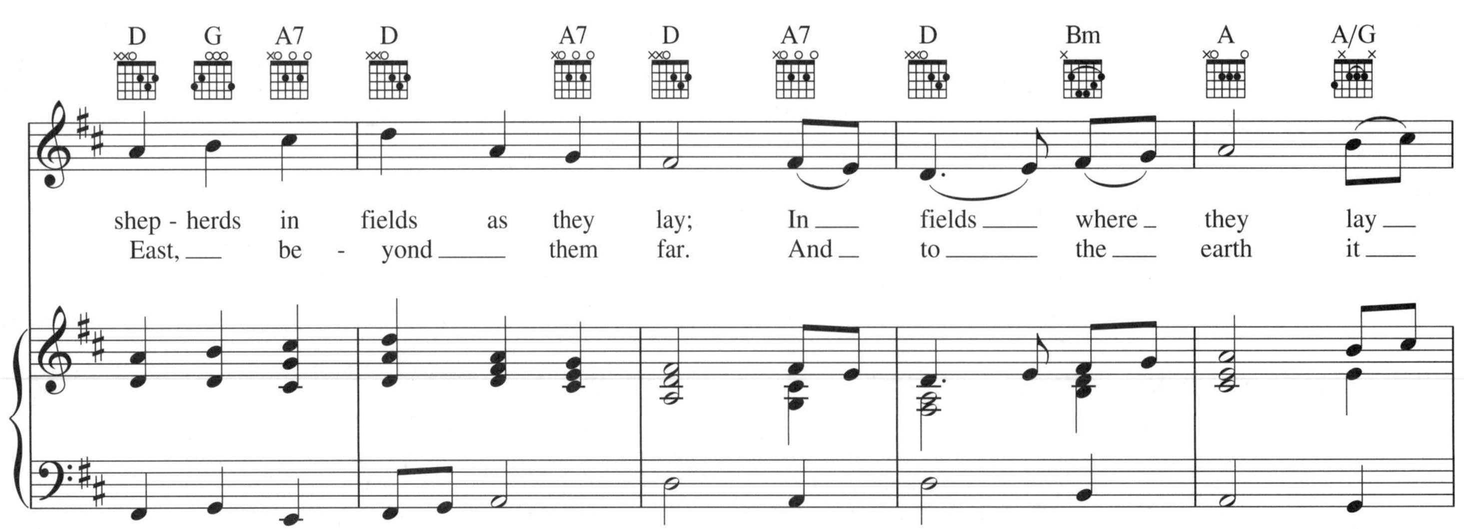

*Additional Lyrics*

3. And by the light of that same star,
   Three wise men came from country far.
   To seek for a King was their intent,
   And to follow the star wherever it went.
   *Refrain*

4. This star drew nigh to the northwest;
   O'er Bethlehem it took its rest.
   And there it did both stop and stay,
   Right over the place where Jesus lay.
   *Refrain*

5. Then entered in those wise men three,
   Full rev'rently upon their knee;
   And offered there in His presence,
   Their gold and myrrh and frankincense.
   *Refrain*

6. Then let us all with one accord
   Sing praises to our heav'nly Lord,
   That hath made heav'n and earth of naught,
   And with His blood mankind hath bought.
   *Refrain*

# THE FRIENDLY BEASTS

Traditional English Carol

*Additional Lyrics*

2. "I," said the donkey, shaggy and brown,
"I carried His mother up hill and down;
I carried her safely to Bethlehem town."
"I," said the donkey, shaggy and brown.

3. "I," said the cow all white and red,
"I gave Him my manger for His bed;
I gave him my hay to pillow His head."
"I," said the cow all white and red.

4. "I," said the sheep with curly horn,
"I gave Him my wool for His blanket warm;
He wore my coat on Christmas morn."
"I," said the sheep with curly horn.

5. "I," said the dove from the rafters high,
"I cooed Him to sleep so He would not cry;
We cooed Him to sleep, my mate and I."
"I," said the dove from the rafters high.

6. Thus every beast by some good spell,
In the stable dark was glad to tell
Of the gift he gave Emmanuel,
The gift he gave Emmanuel.

# FROM THE EASTERN MOUNTAINS

Words by GODFREY THRING
Traditional Melody

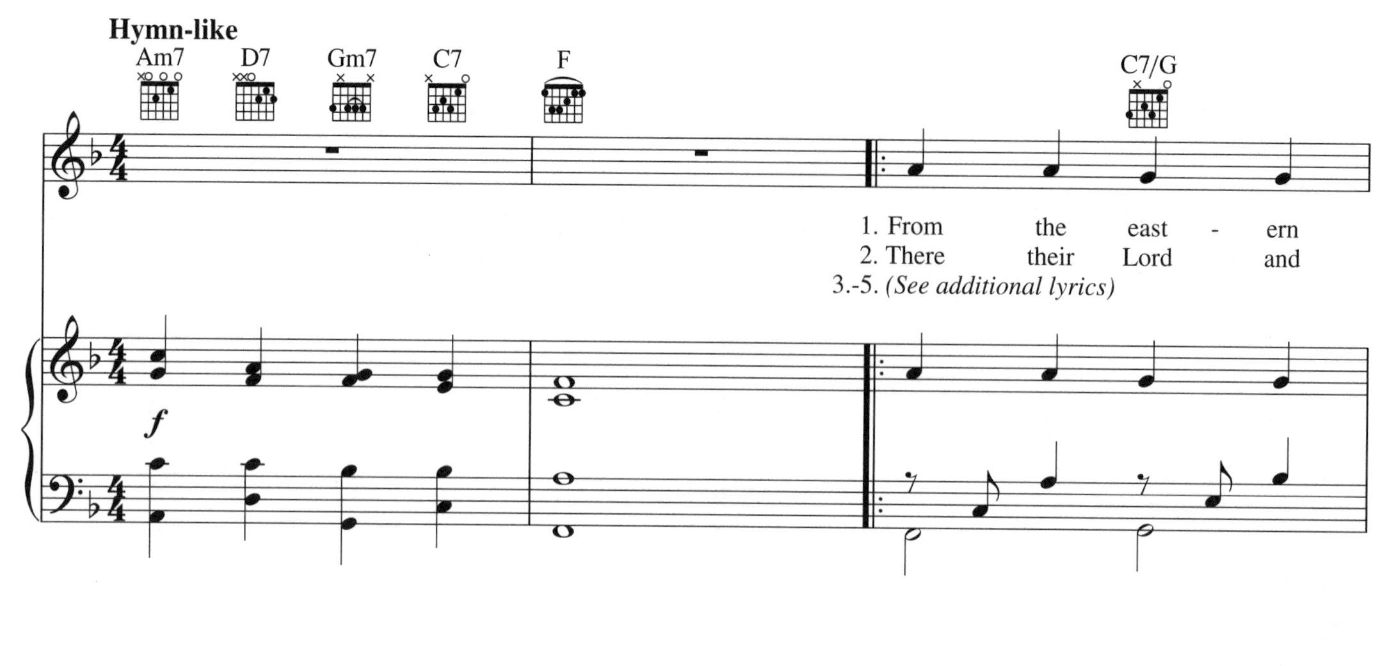


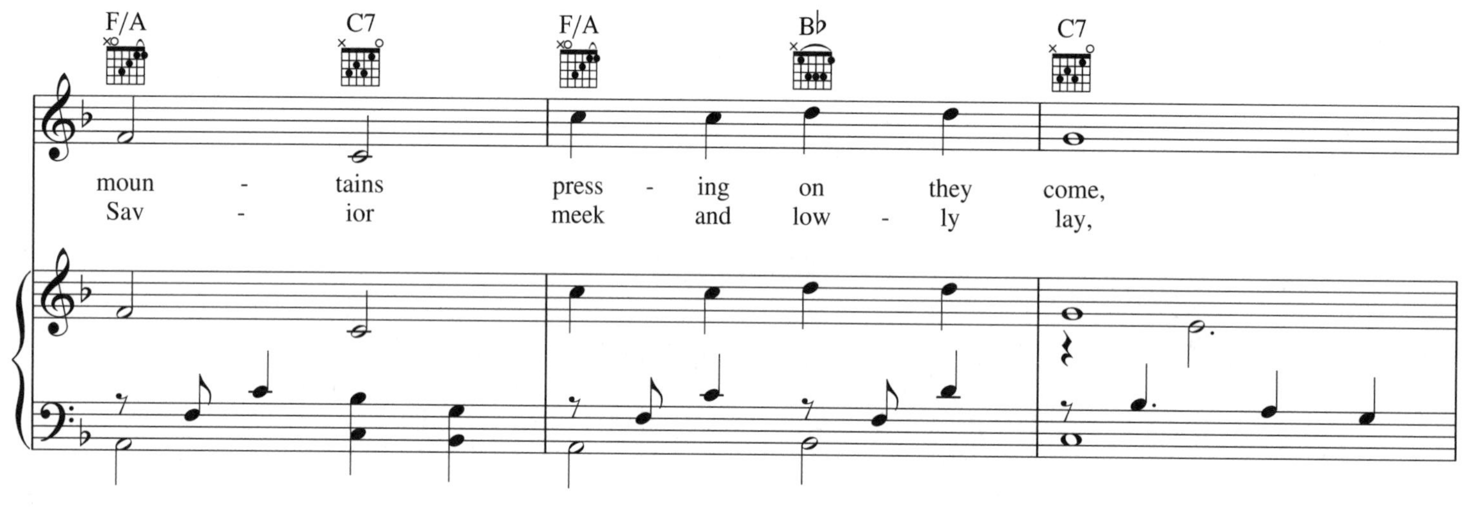


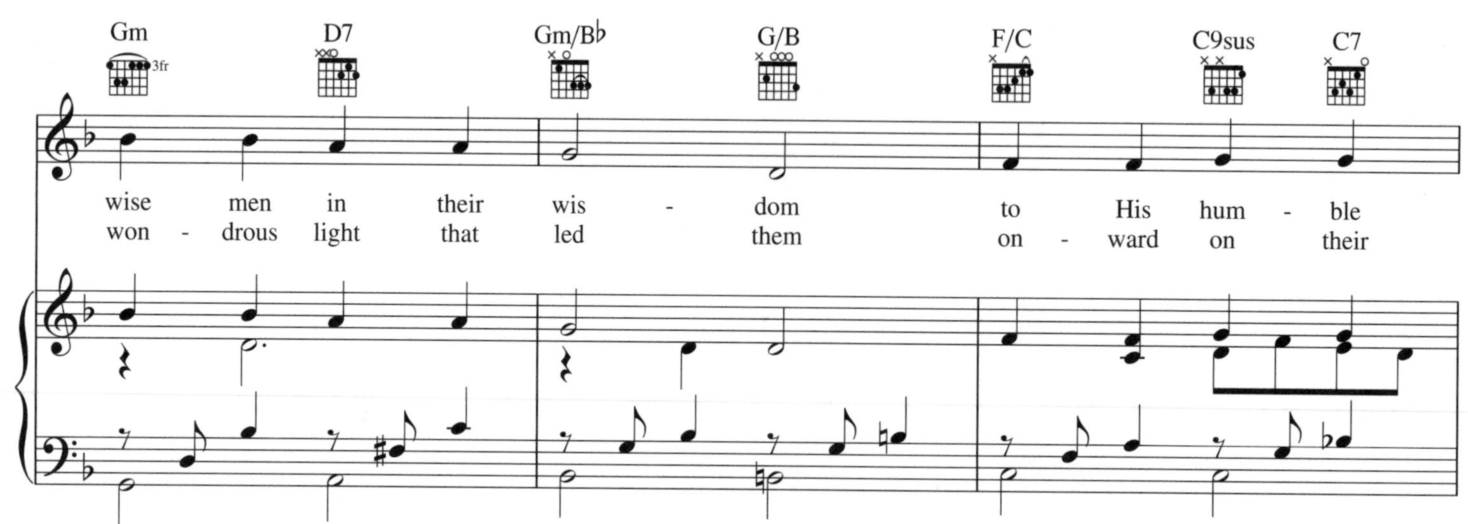

*Additional Lyrics*

3. Thou who in a manger
Once hast lowly lain,
Who dost now in glory
O'er all kingdoms reign,
Gather in the heathen
Who in lands afar
Ne'er have seen the brightness
Of Thy guiding star.

4. Gather in the outcasts,
All who have astray,
Throw Thy radiance o'er them,
Guide them on their way,
Those who never knew Thee,
Those who have wandered far,
Guide them by the brightness
Of Thy guiding star.

5. Onward through the darkness
Of the lonely night,
Shining still before them
With Thy kindly light,
Guide them, Jew and Gentile,
Homeward from afar,
Young and old together,
By thy guiding star.

# FUM, FUM, FUM

Traditional Catalonian Carol

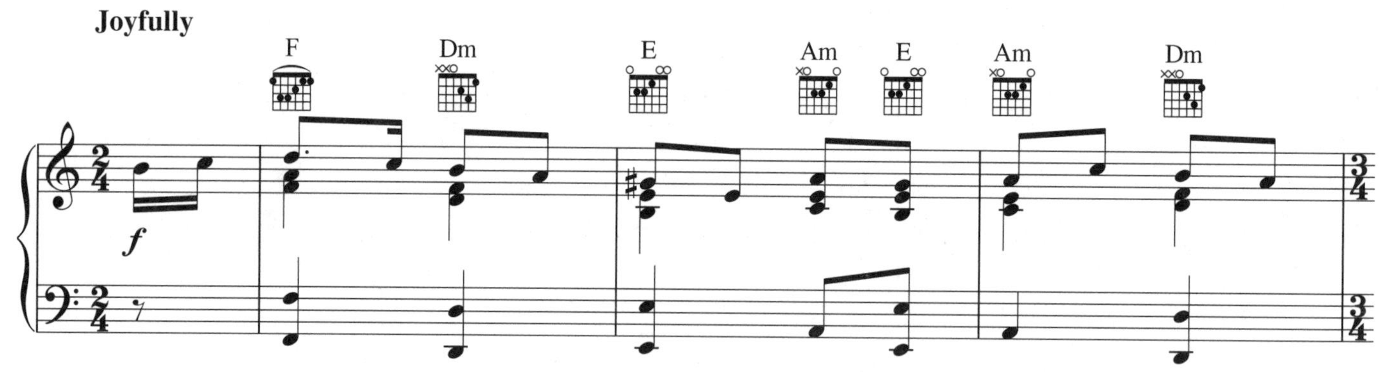

Am E Am C Fdim7/C C
Fum, Fum, Fum. For a bless - ed Babe was born up - on this
Fdim7/C C F Dm
day at break of morn. In a man - ger poor and
E Am E Am Dm E Am E
low - ly lay the Son of God most ho - ly, Fum, Fum,
Am Dm E Am E
Fum. Thanks to God for hol - i - days, sing Fum, Fum,

Am
Dm
E
Am
E
Fum. Thanks to God for hol - i - days, sing Fum, Fum,
Am
C
Fdim7/C
C
Fdim7/C
Fum. Now we all our voic - es raise and sing a song of grate - ful
C
F
Dm
E
Am
E
praise. Cel - e - brate in song and sto - ry all the
Am
Dm
E
Am
E
Am
won - ders of His glo - ry, Fum, Fum, Fum.

# GLORIA

Traditional Austrian Carol

# GATHER AROUND THE CHRISTMAS TREE

Words and Music by
JOHN H. HOPKINS

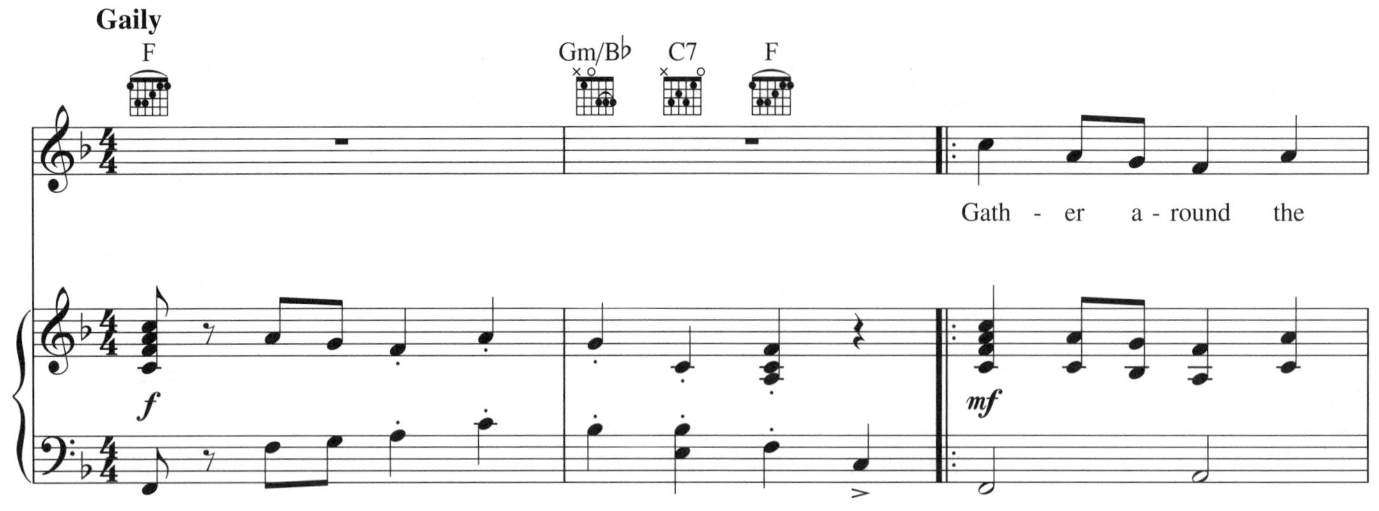

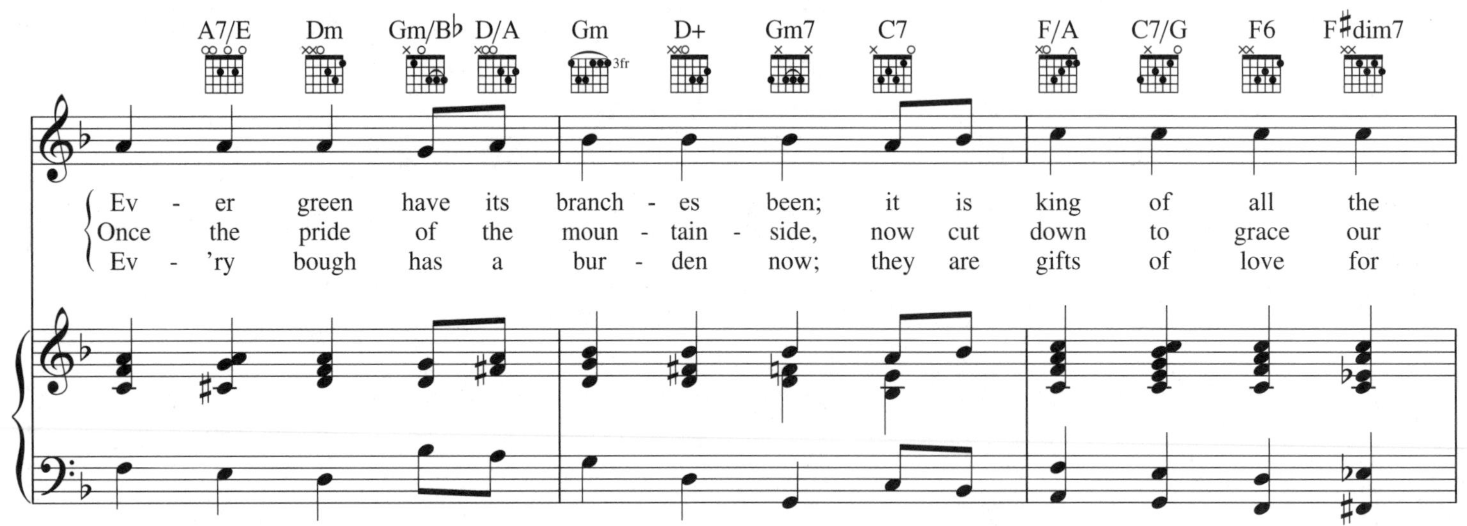

C/G G7 C F♯dim7 C7/G Gm/F C/E Gm7/D C♯dim7 Dm F7/C
wood - land scene. For Christ our King is born to - day! His
Christ - mas - tide. For Christ from Heav'n to earth came down to
us, we trow. For Christ is born, His love to show, and
Bm7♭5 B♭6 Am7 Fm6/A♭ C/G G7/B C F♯dim7 Gm7 Gm7/B♭ D7/A
reign shall nev - er pass a - way.
gain, through death, a no - bler crown.
give good gifts to men be - low.
Ho - san - na, ho -
Gm7 B♭m6 F/A Dm7 Gm7 F/A C9 F
san - na, ho - san - na in the high - est!
Gm/B♭ C7 F Gm/B♭ C7 F
Gath - er a - round the Christ - mas tree! Gath - er a - round the Christ - mas tree!
3fr
6fr

# GO, TELL IT ON THE MOUNTAIN

African-American Spiritual
Verses by JOHN W. WORK, JR.

G
G6
Gmaj7
G7
C6
Cm6/E♭
shep - herds kept their watch - ing o'er si - lent flocks by
shep - herds feared and trem - bled when, lo! a - bove the
in a low - ly man - ger the hum - ble Christ was
G
Am7
G
G6
Gmaj7
G7
night, Be - hold, through - out the heav - ens, there
earth Rang out the an - gel cho - rus that
born, And God sent us sal - va - tion that
Em7
A7
1, 2
D7sus
D7
3
D7sus
D7
D.S. al Coda
shone a ho - ly light.
hailed our Sav - ior's birth.
bless - ed Christ - mas morn.
CODA
G/D
D7
G
C/G
G
Je - sus Christ is born.

# GOD REST YE MERRY, GENTLEMEN

19th Century English Carol

Gm C F B♭ F7/A B♭ F A7 Dm G/D C F
3fr
3fr
save us all from Sa - tan's pow'r when we were gone a -
which His moth - er Mar - y did noth - ing take in
that in Beth - le - hem was born the Son of God by
went to Beth - le - hem straight - way, the Son of God to
C Dm C/E F B♭ F C7/G Dm/A A
stray.
scorn.
name.
find.
O tid - ings of com - fort and
Dm G7 C F B♭
joy, com - fort and joy; O tid - ings of
F C7/G Dm/A A
1-3
Dm
4
Dm
com - fort and joy!
In
From
The
joy!

# GOING TO BETHLEHEM

Traditional Chilean Carol

C D A D
fer - vent prayer I am of - f'ring, a fer - vent prayer I am of - f'ring.
rich from wool you'll be sell - ing, so rich from wool you'll be sell - ing. Go - ing,
love and glo - ry be - hold - ing, thy love and glo - ry be - hold - ing.
G D7 G
go - ing to Beth - le - hem town, go - ing, go - ing the ba - by to see, to
To Coda
1
C D A D
greet his fa - ther, Jo - seph, and Mar - y, on bend - ed knee. Go - ing,
2
A D7 G
Mar - y, on bend - ed knee.
D.C.
CODA
A D7 G
Mar - y, on bend - ed knee.

# GOOD CHRISTIAN MEN, REJOICE

14th Century Latin Text
Translated by JOHN MASON NEALE
14th Century German Melody

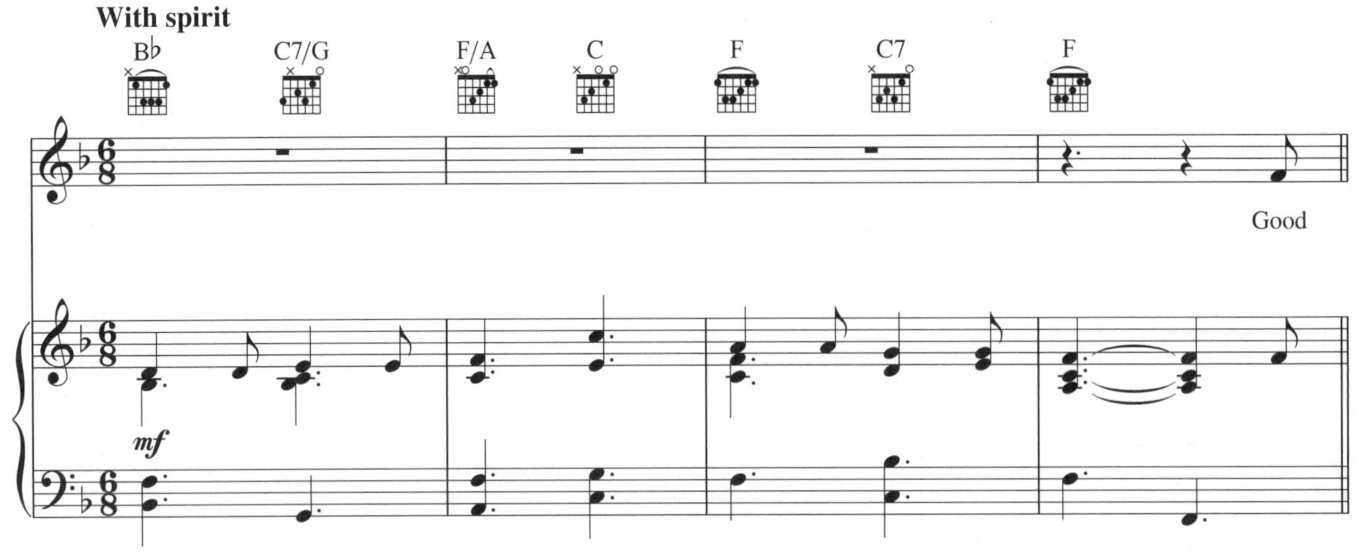

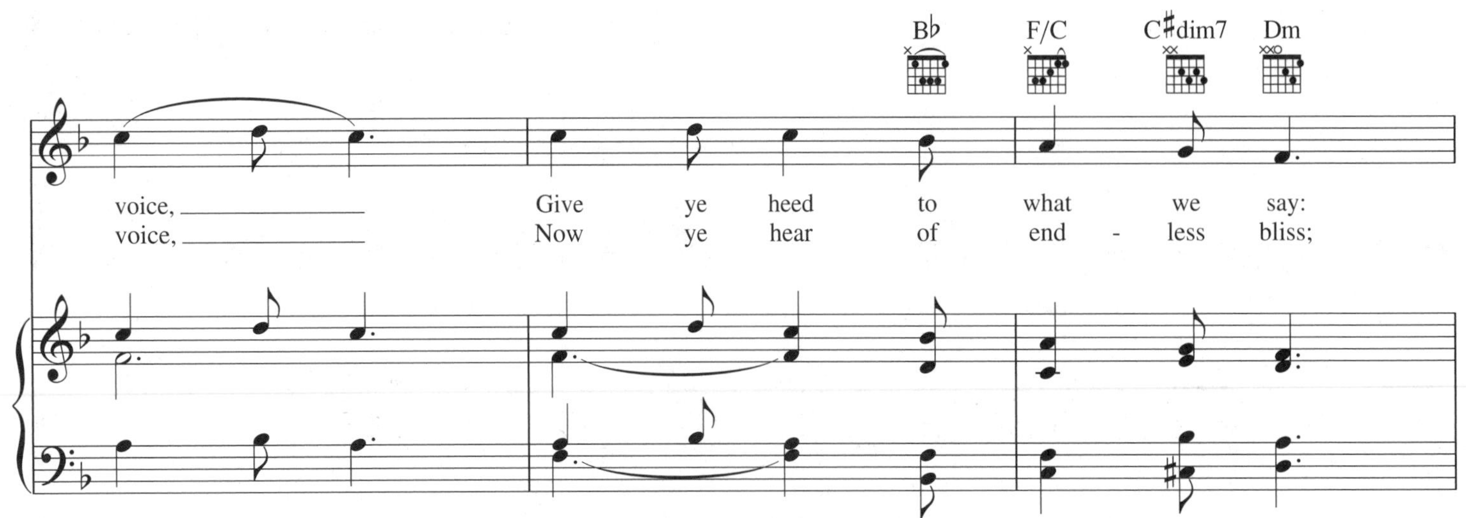

B♭ F/A Gm7 C7 Dm C F
News! News! Je - sus Christ is born to - day!
Joy! Joy! Je - sus Christ was born for this.
B♭ F/C C♯dim7 Dm Gm7 C7
Ox and ass be - fore Him bow, And He is in the
He hath ope'd the heav'n - ly door, And man is bless - ed
Dm C F B♭ C7/G F/A C
man - ger now; Christ is born to - day!
ev - er - more. Christ was born for this!
F C7 1 F 2 F
Christ is born to - day. Good
Christ was born for this!

# GOOD KING WENCESLAS

Words by JOHN M. NEALE
Music from *Piae Cantiones*

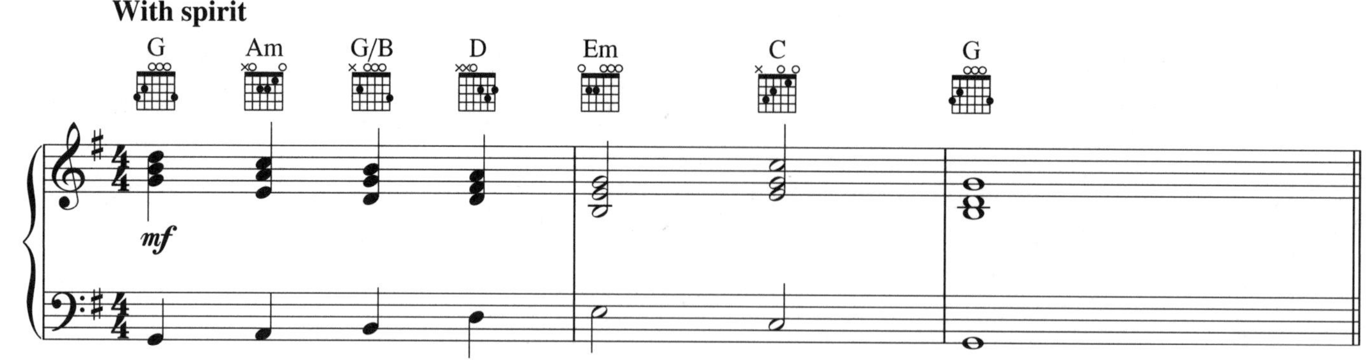


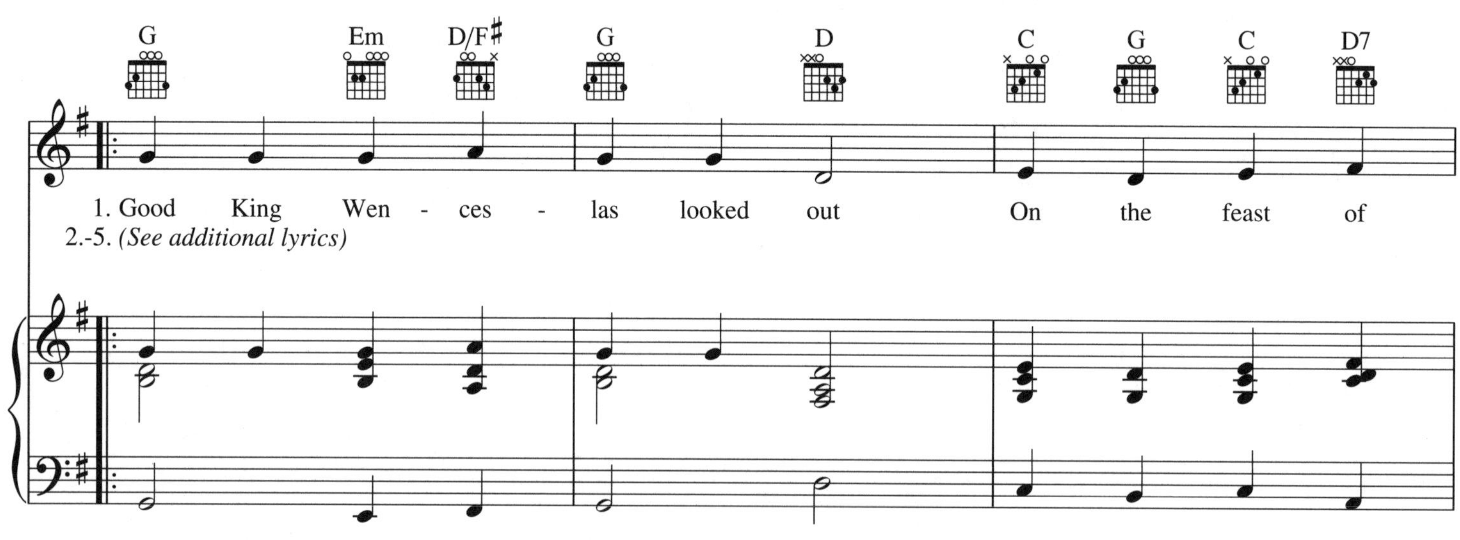


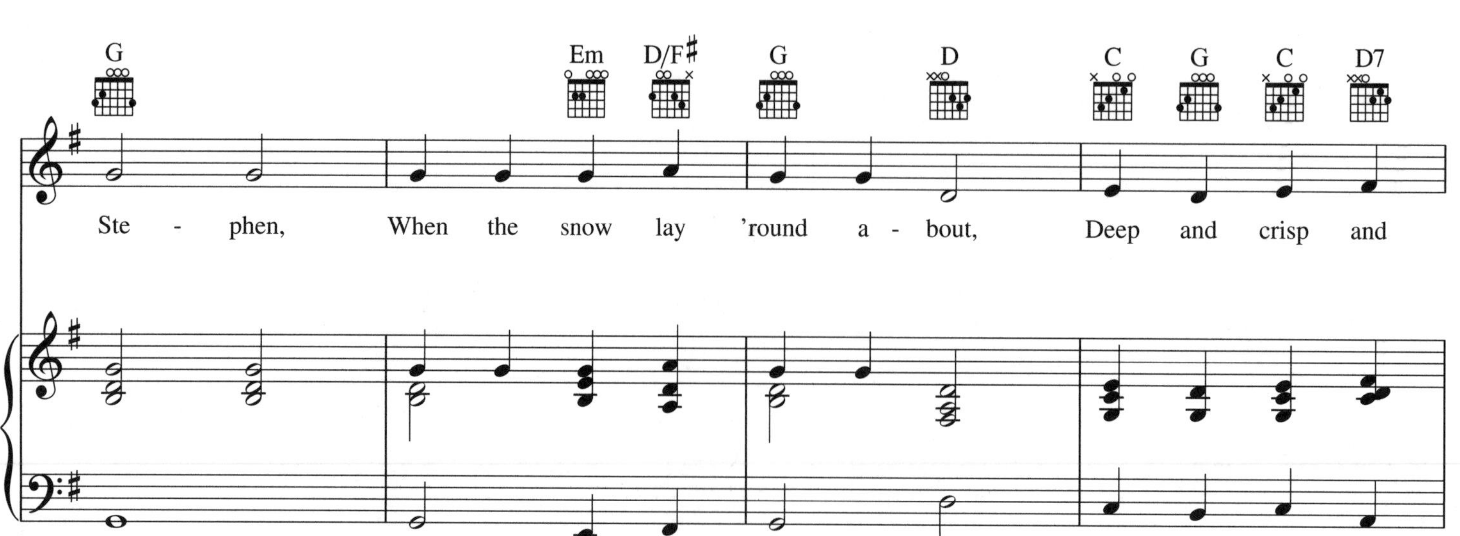

*Additional Lyrics*

2. "Hither page, and stand by me,
If thou know'st it, telling,
Yonder peasant, who is he?
Where and what his dwelling?"
"Sire, he lives a good league hence,
Underneath the mountain;
Right against the forest fence,
By Saint Agnes' fountain."

3. "Bring me flesh, and bring me wine,
Bring me pine-logs hither;
Thou and I will see him dine,
When we bear them thither."
Page and monarch forth they went,
Forth they went together;
Through the rude wind's wild lament
And the bitter weather.

4. "Sire, the night is darker now,
And the wind blows stronger;
Fails my heart, I know not how,
I can go no longer."
"Mark my footsteps, my good page,
Tred thou in them boldly:
Thou shalt find the winter's rage
Freeze thy blood less coldly."

5. In his master's steps he trod,
Where the snow lay dinted;
Heat was in the very sod
Which the saint had printed.
Therefore, Christian men, be sure,
Wealth or rank possessing,
Ye who now will bless the poor,
Shall yourselves find blessing.

# HARK! THE HERALD ANGELS SING

Words by CHARLES WESLEY
Altered by GEORGE WHITEFIELD
Music by FELIX MENDELSSOHN-BARTHOLDY
Arranged by WILLIAM H. CUMMINGS

G
D7/F♯
G/D
D
C
E7/B
Am
E7
D7
G/B
Joy - ful all ye na - tions rise, Join the tri - umph of the skies; With th' an - gel - ic host pro - claim,
Veiled in flesh the God - head see; Hail th' In - car - nate De - i - ty, Pleased as Man with men to dwell,
Mild He lays His glo - ry by, Born that man no more may die, Born to raise the sons of earth,
"Christ is born in Beth - le - hem."
Je - sus our Em - man - u - el!
Born to give them sec - ond birth.
Hark! The her - ald an - gels sing, "Glo - ry to the new - born King!"

# HE IS BORN

## (Il est ne, le divin enfant)

Traditional French Carol

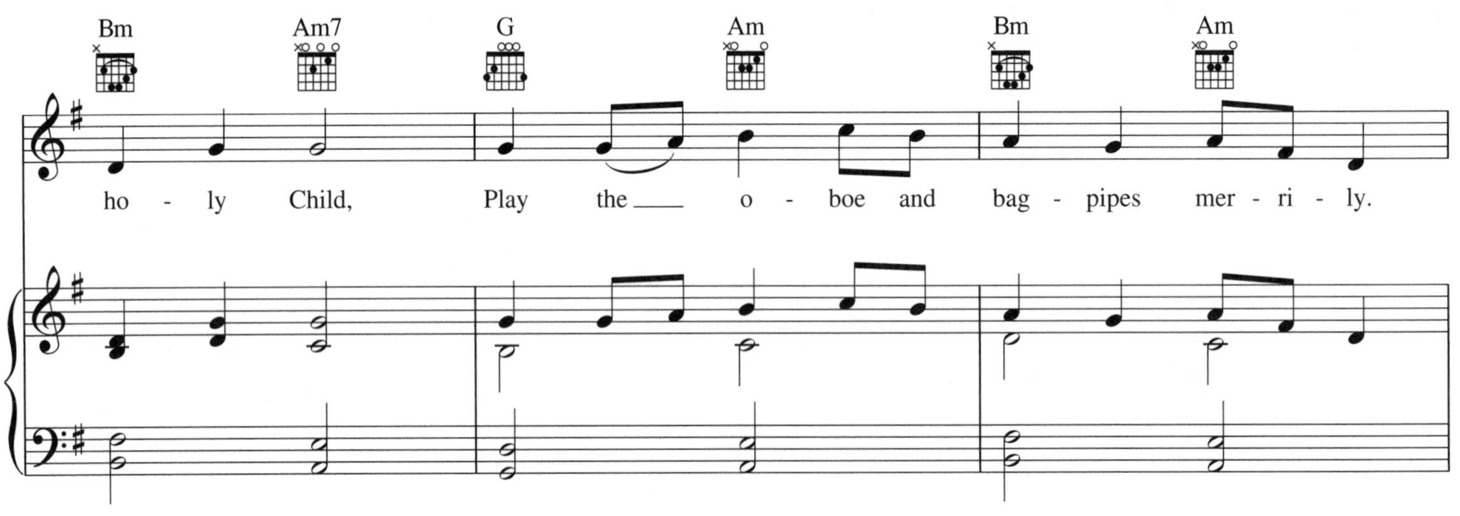


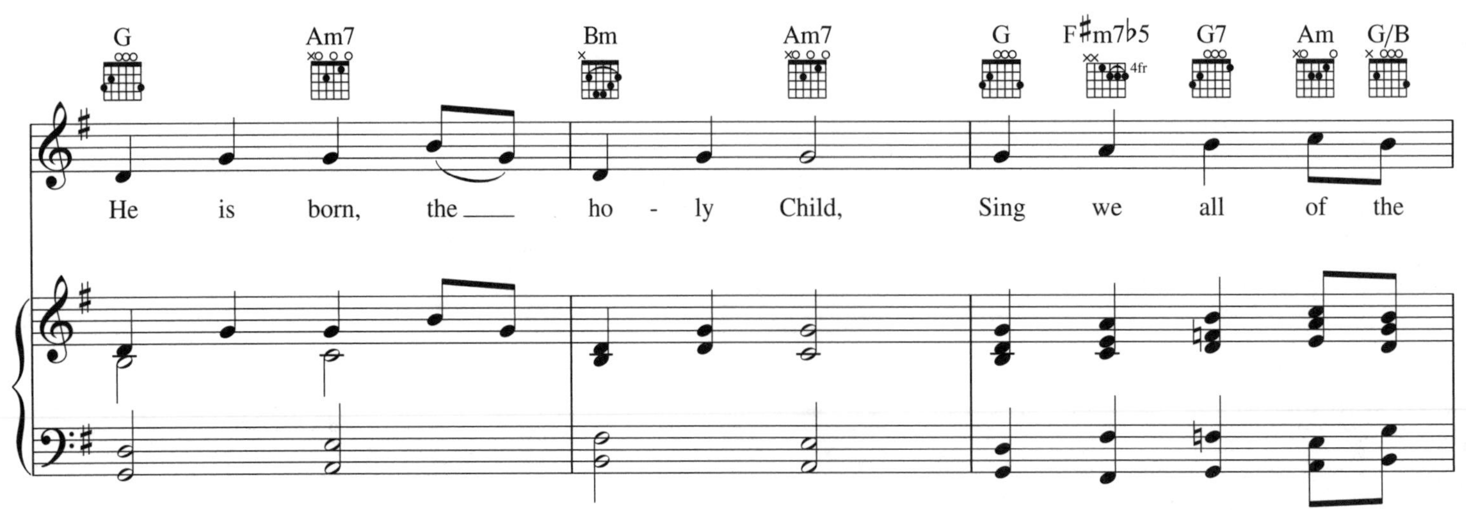

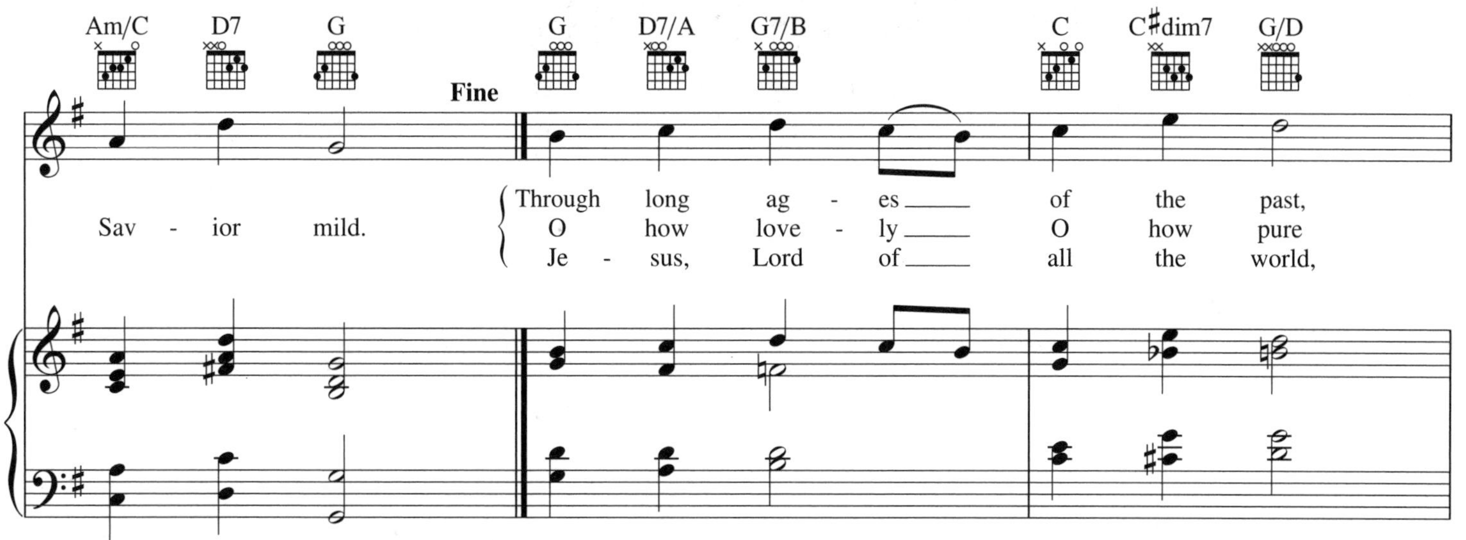

Am/C D7 G G D7/A G7/B C C♯dim7 G/D
Fine
Sav - ior mild.
Through long ag - es of the past,
O how love - ly O how pure
Je - sus, Lord of all the world,


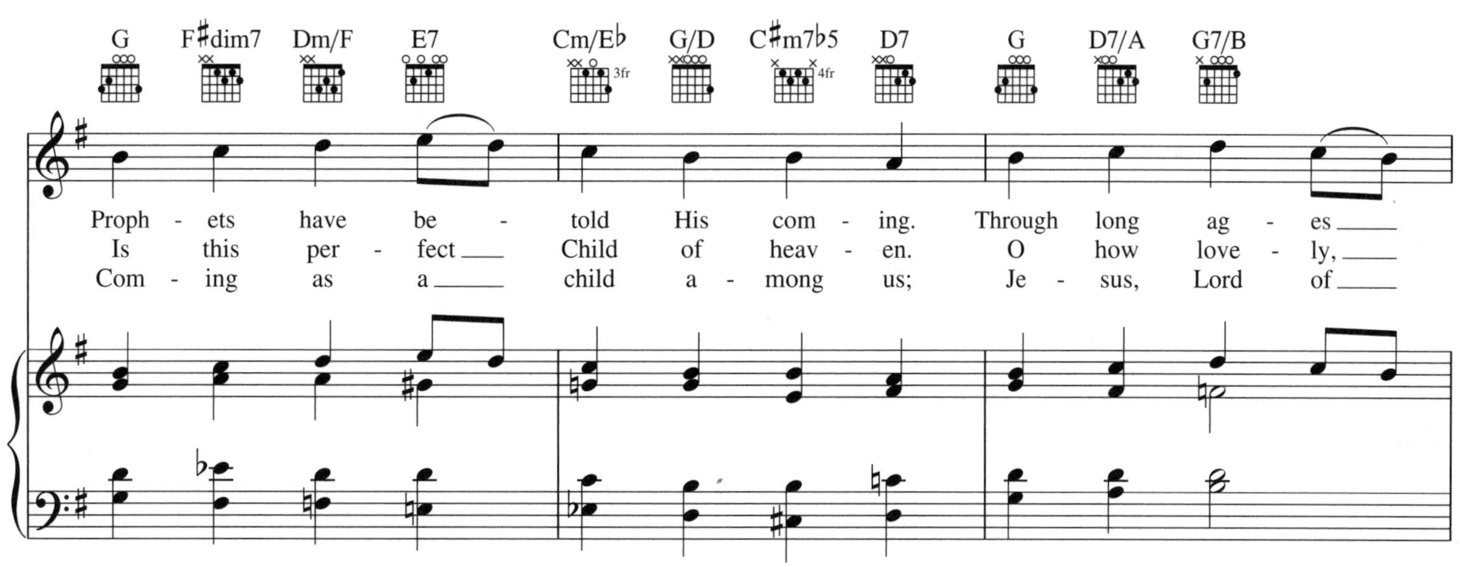

G F♯dim7 Dm/F E7 Cm/E♭ G/D C♯m7♭5 D7 G D7/A G7/B
3fr
4fr
Proph - ets have be - told His com - ing. Through long ag - es
Is this per - fect Child of heav - en. O how love - ly,
Com - ing as a child a - mong us; Je - sus, Lord of


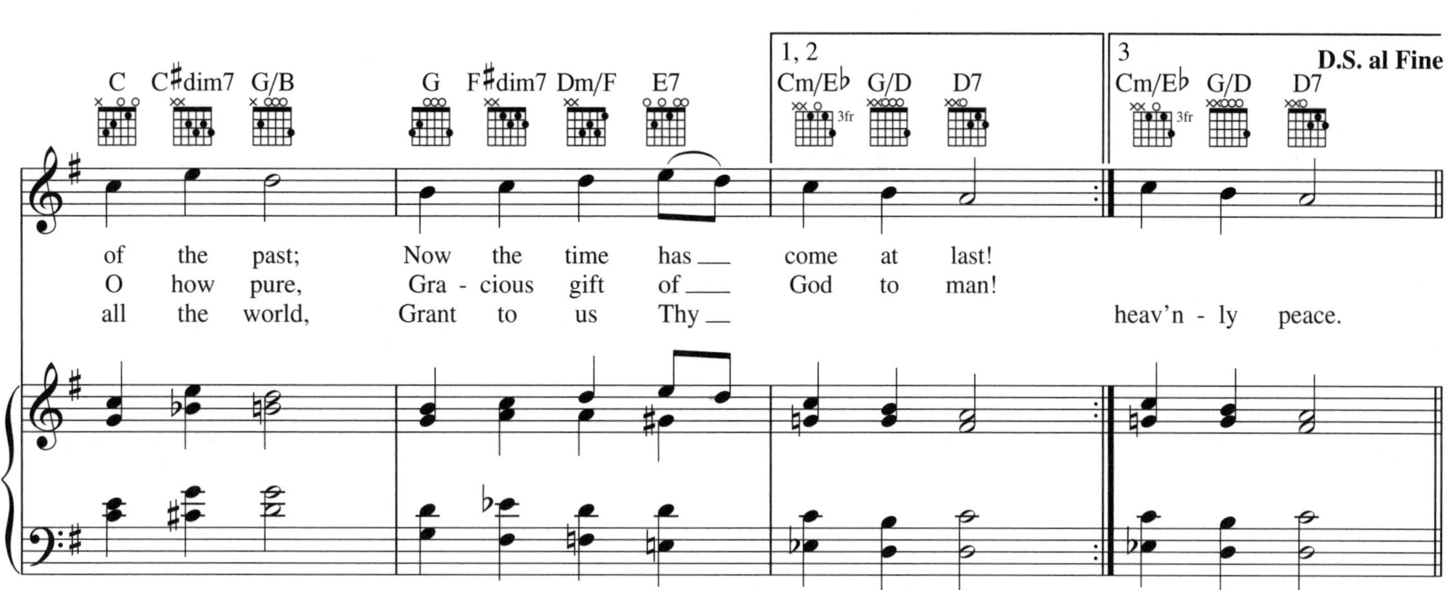

1, 2
3
D.S. al Fine
C C♯dim7 G/B G F♯dim7 Dm/F E7 Cm/E♭ G/D D7 Cm/E♭ G/D D7
3fr
3fr
of the past; Now the time has come at last!
O how pure, Gra - cious gift of God to man!
all the world, Grant to us Thy heav'n - ly peace.

# HEAR THEM BELLS

Words and Music by
D.S. McCOSH

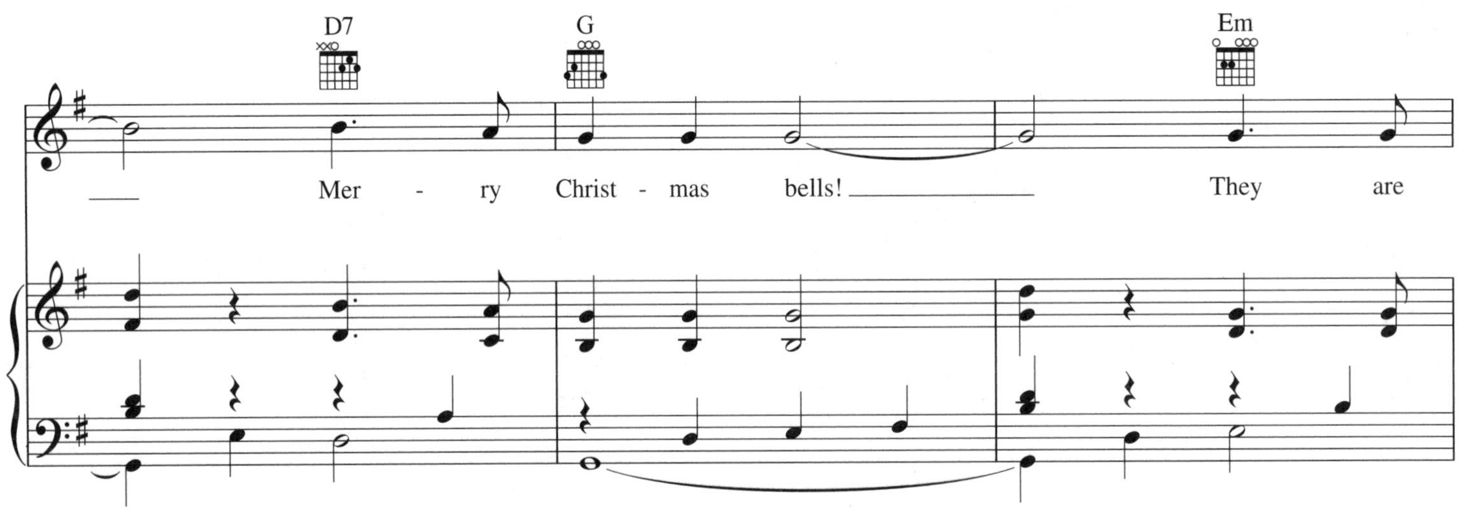


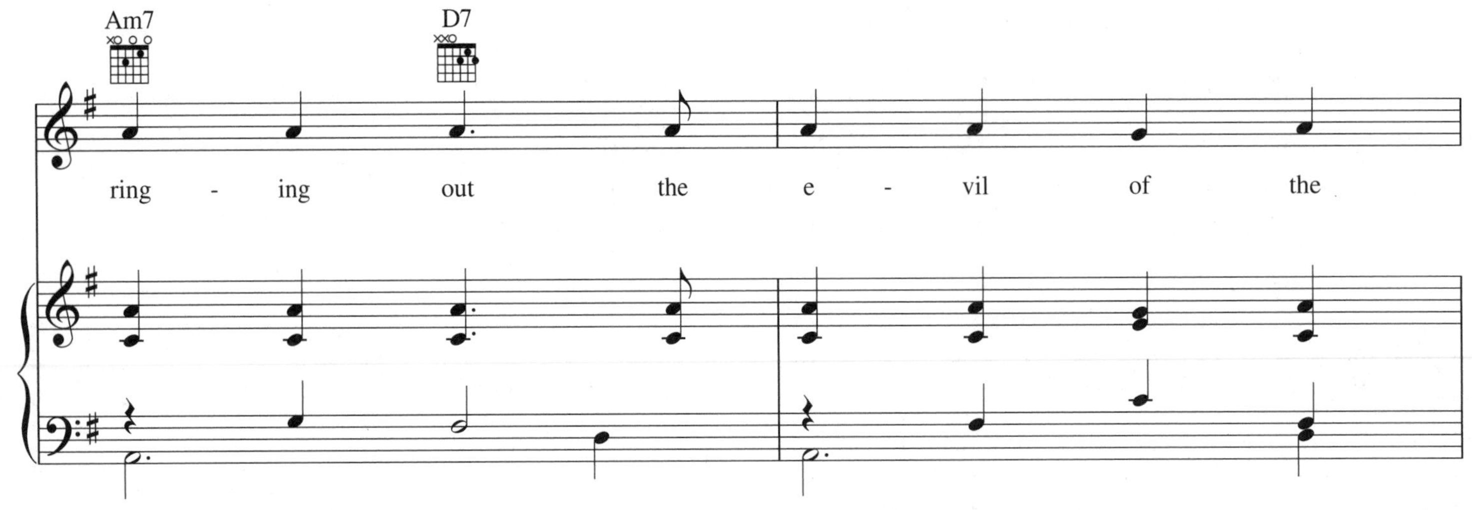

G
sword;
Hear them bells!
D7
G
Mer - ry Christ - mas bells!
Em
Am7
D7
They are ring - ing in the
Am7
D7
G
D7
G
glo - ry of the Lord!

# THE HOLLY AND THE IVY

18th Century English Carol

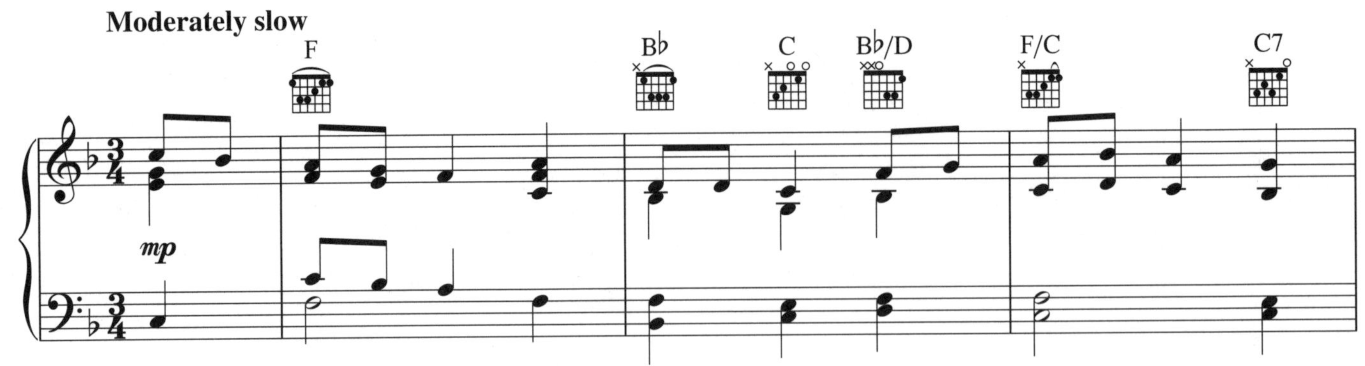


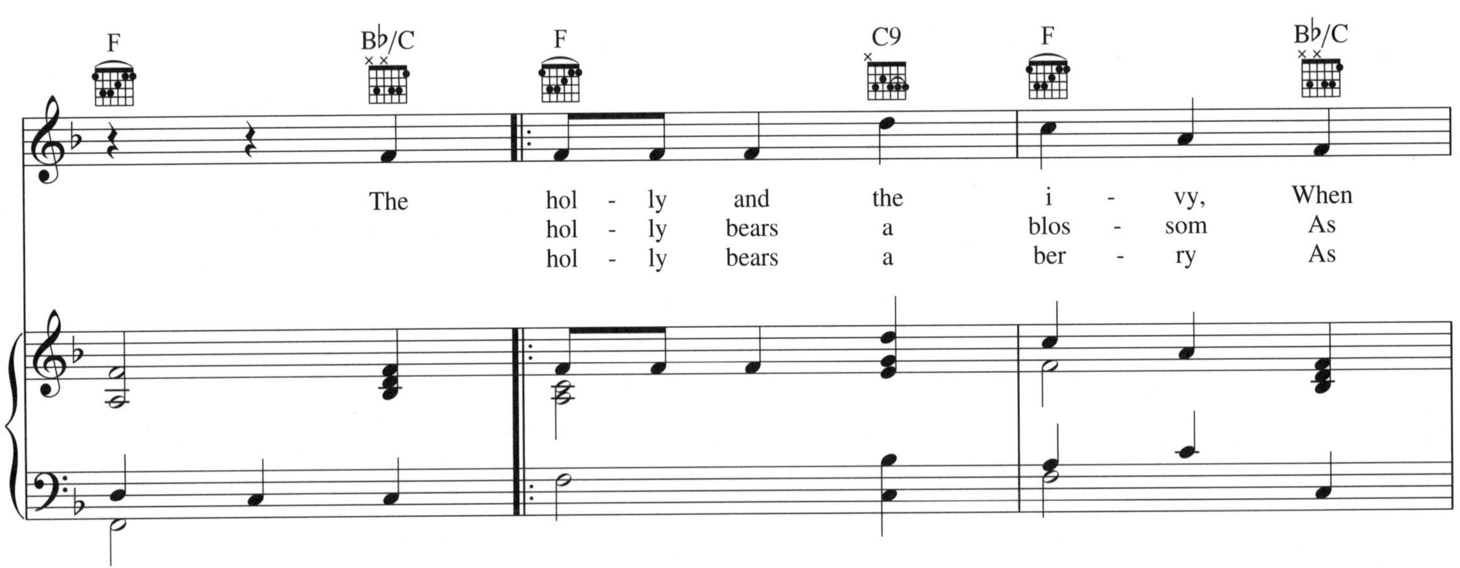


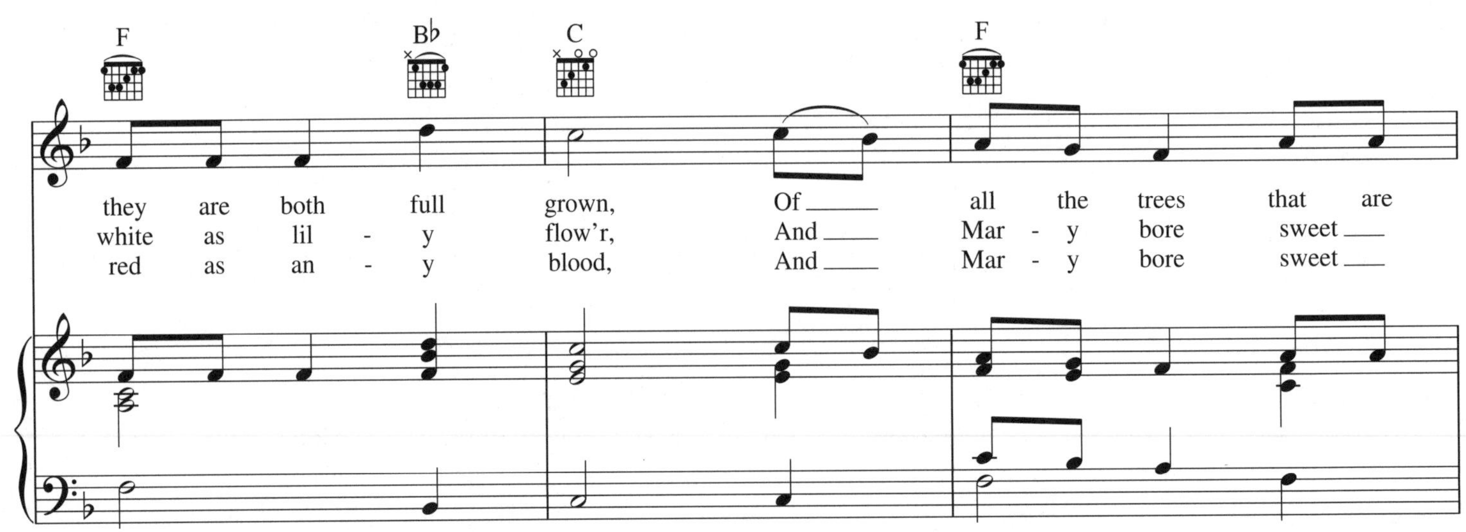

B♭
C
B♭/D
F/C
C7
F
B♭/C
in the wood, The ___ hol - ly bears the crown.
Je - sus Christ To ___ be our sweet Sav - ior. The
Je - sus Christ To ___ do poor sin - ners good.
F
C9
F
B♭/C
F
B♭
ris - ing of the sun ___ And the run - ning of the
C
F
B♭
C
B♭/D
deer, The ___ play - ing of the mer - ry or - gan, sweet
F/C
C7
1, 2
F
3
F
sing - ing of the choir. The choir.

# HOW BRIGHTLY BEAMS THE MORNING STAR

Words and Music by PHILIPP NICOLAI
Translated by WILLIAM MERCER
Harmonized by J.S. BACH

Bm
D9
4fr
Bm
E
A
Bm
F♯
Bm
A/C♯
ness of God, that breaks our night. And fills the dark - en'd
heart doth praise Thee o'er and o'er, if Thou art mine I
E
A
D
G
D
Em
D
Asus
A
D
souls with light, who long for truth were pin - ing!
ask no more, be wealth or fame de - nied me.
G
A
D
A
D
Asus
A
Thy word, Je - su, in - ly feeds us,
Thee I seek now, none who proves Thee,
D
Asus
A
D
A
1-4
D
right - ly leads us, life be - stow - ing; Praise, oh,
none who loves Thee, finds Thee fail him; Lord of

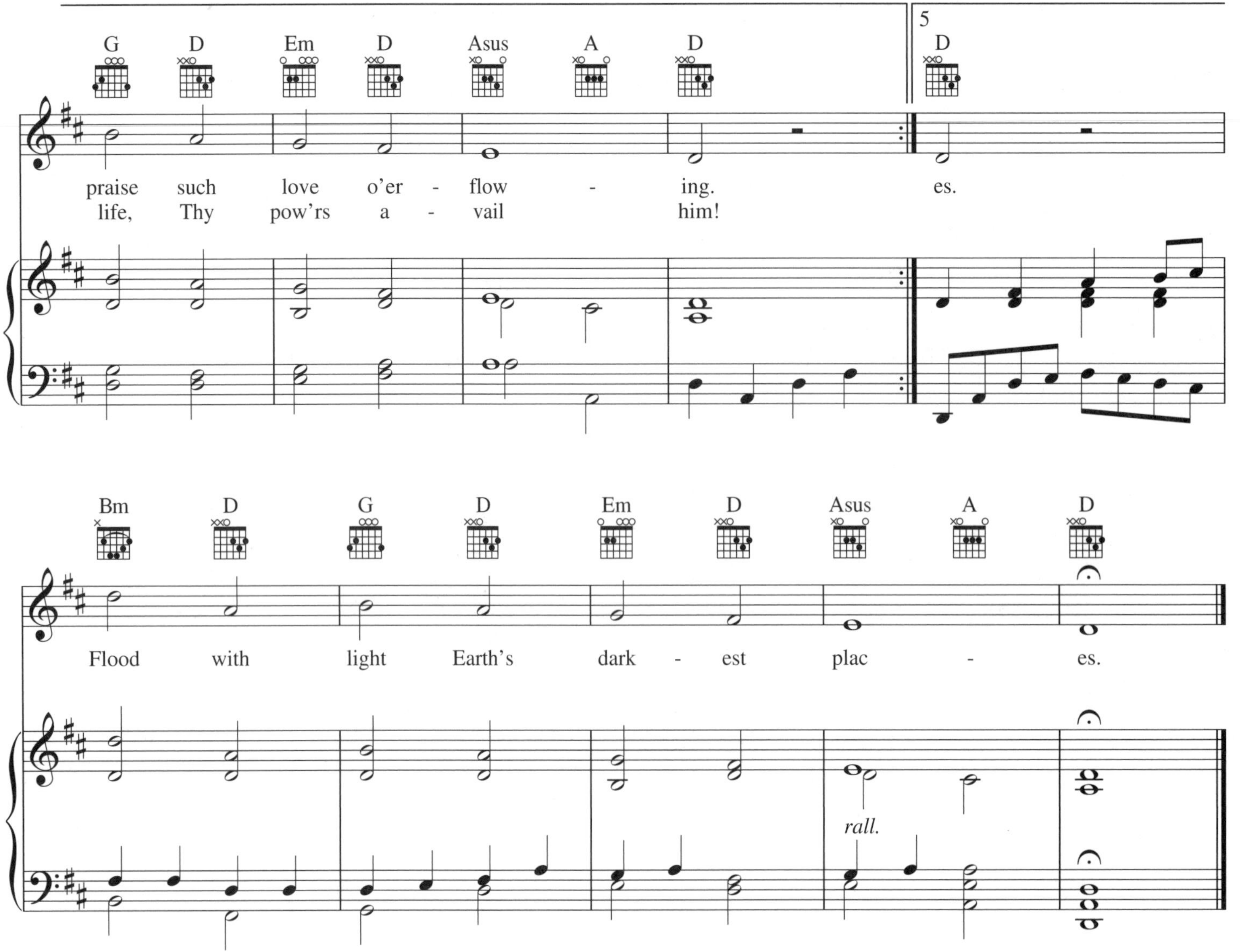


*Additional Lyrics*

3. Through Thee alone can I be blest,
Then deep be on my heart imprest
The love that Thou has borne me;
So make it ready to fulfill
With burning zeal Thy holy will,
Though men may vex or scorn me;
Saviour, let me
Never lose Thee,
For I choose Thee,
Thirst to know Thee;
All I am and have I owe Thee!

4. O God, our Father far above,
Thee, too, I praise, for all the love
Thou in Thy Son dost give me!
In Him am I made one with Thee,
My Brother and my Friend is He;
Shall aught affright or grieve me?
He is Greatest,
Best, and Highest,
Ever nighest
To the weakest;
Fear no foes, if Him thou seekest!

5. O praise to Him who come to save,
Who conquer'd death and burst the grave;
Each day new praise resoundeth
To Him the Lamb who once was slain,
The Friend whom none shall trust in vain,
Whose grace for aye aboundeth;
Sing, ye Heavens,
Tell the story
Of His glory,
Till His praises
Flood with light Earth's darkest places.

# I AM SO GLAD ON CHRISTMAS EVE

Words by MARIE WEXELSEN
Music by PEDER KNUDSEN

# I GO TO BETHLEHEM

Traditional Czech Carol

B♭7
E♭
3fr
give ___ Him.
give ___ Him.
Coo, coo - coo!
Coo, coo - coo!
B♭7
E♭
3fr
Je - sus, ___ he ___ sings for You!
Coo, coo - coo!
B♭7
E♭
B♭
E♭
Coo, coo - coo!
Je - sus, ___ he ___ sings for You!
B♭7
E♭

# I HEARD THE BELLS ON CHRISTMAS DAY

Words by HENRY WADSWORTH LONGFELLOW
Music by JOHN BAPTISTE CALKIN

*Additional Verses*

3. And in despair I bowed my head:
"There is no peace on earth," I said,
"For hate is strong, and mocks the song
Of peace on earth, good will to men."

4. Then pealed the bells more loud and deep:
"God is not dead, nor doth He sleep;
The wrong shall fail, the right prevail,
With peace on earth, good will to men."

5. Till, ringing, singing on its way,
The world revolved from night to day,
A voice, a chime, a chant sublime,
Of peace on earth, good will to men!

# I SAW THREE SHIPS

Traditional English Carol

# IN BETHLEHEM, THE LOWLY

Traditional Dutch Carol

G
Am
E
Am
will I wor - ship on - ly, while
with a thou - sand voic - es, my
D
G
D
on this earth I stay.
praise to Him I sing.
G/B
D
G/B
D
Oh! Yes! Oh! Yes! Je -
Oh! Yes! Oh! Yes! He
G
D7
1
G
2
G
sus was born this day. My
is my Lord and King.

# IN BETHLEHEM'S CRADLE

Traditional Puerto Rican Carol

C7
F
C7
Je - sus, of the dear Ba - by, O what a glo - rious gift from a -
F
C7
F
bove! He has our hearts and all of our love! He has our
F
C7
F
hearts and all of our love! Le - rum, le - rum, le - rum,
1 - 3
4
la!
There with -
To His
Al - so

# INFANT HOLY, INFANT LOWLY

Traditional Polish Carol

G
G/B
Cmaj7
C6
D
D7
B/D♯
4fr
all. Swift are wing - ing an - gels sing - ing, no - ëls
Em7
C/E
D/F♯
D
D7/C
G/B
C
D7
ring - ing, tid - ings bring - ing: Christ the Babe is Lord of
G
E♭maj7
3fr
F
G6/9
all!
G
D7/G
Flocks are sleep - ing, shep - herds keep - ing vig - il

G/B C Bm/D B7/D♯ Em C D7/A G

till the morn - ing new saw the glo - ry, heard the

D7/G G/B C D7 G G/B Cmaj7 C6

sto - ry, tid - ings of a Gos - pel true. Thus re - joic - ing, free from

D B/D♯ Em C/E Cm/E♭ D D7/C

4fr 3fr

sor - row, prais - es voic - ing greet the mor - row: Christ the

*cresc.*

G7/B C D7 G6/9 G(add9)

Babe was born for you.

*poco rit.* *a tempo*

# IT CAME UPON THE MIDNIGHT CLEAR

Words by EDMUND HAMILTON SEARS
Music by RICHARD STORRS WILLIS

E♭
Cm7
F7
B♭
earth To touch their harps of gold:
floats O'er all the wea - ry world.
rolled Two thou - sand years of wrong.
N.C.
D
D/C
Gm/B♭
D
"Peace on the earth, good will to
A - bove its sad and low - ly
And man, at war with man, hears
Gm
F/C
C7
F
men, From heav'n's all gra - cious King."
plains, They bend on hov - 'ring wing,
not The love song which they bring.
F7
B♭
B♭+
E♭/B♭
B♭
The world in sol - emn still - ness
And ev - er o'er its Ba - bel
O hush the noise, ye men of

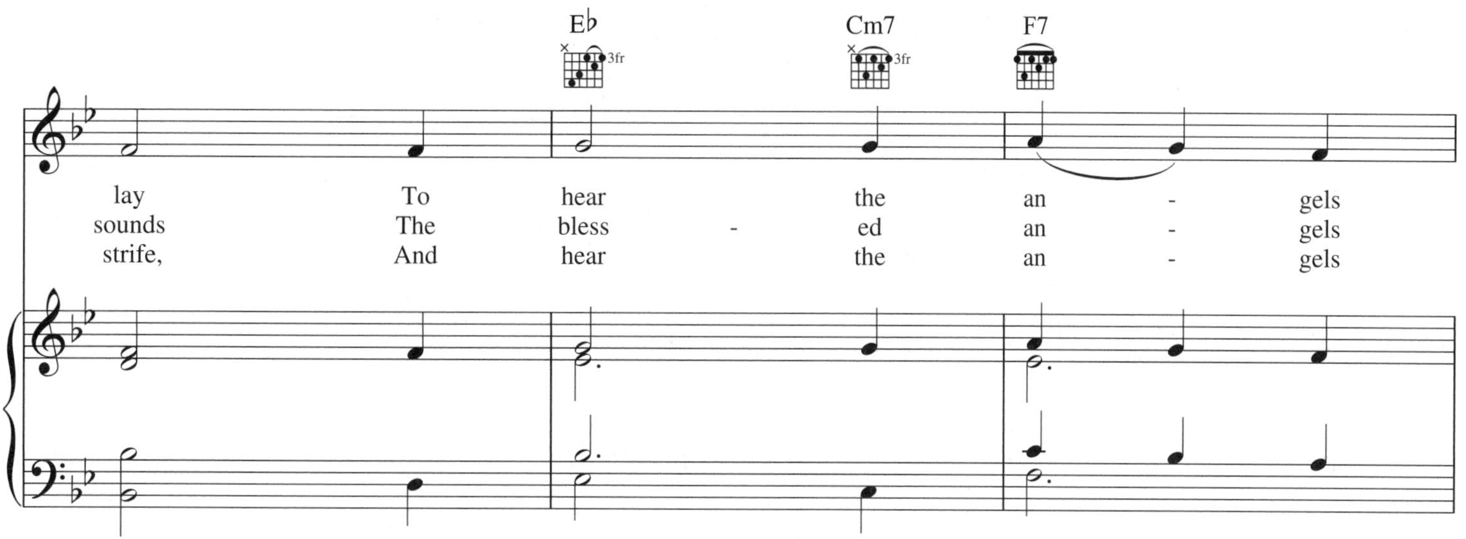


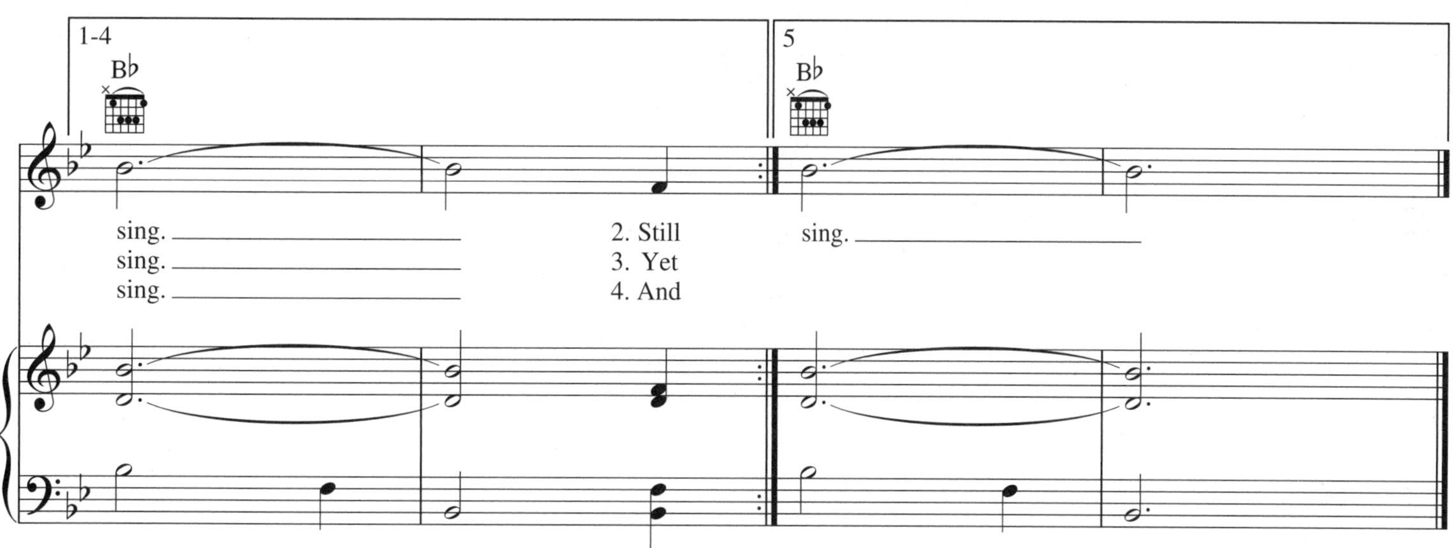


*Additional Lyrics*

4. And ye, beneath life's crushing load,
   Whose forms are bending low,
   Who toil along the climbing way
   With painful steps and slow,
   Look now! for glad and golden hours
   Come swiftly on the wing.
   O rest beside the weary road,
   And hear the angels sing.

5. For lo! the days are hast'ning on,
   By prophet-bards foretold.
   When, with the ever-circling years,
   Shall come the Age of Gold,
   When peace shall over all the earth
   Its heav'nly splendors fling,
   And all the world give back the song
   Which now the angels sing.

# INFANT SO GENTLE

Traditional French Carol

B♭
E♭
3fr
Fm
B♭
Ten - d'rest words fail all Thy beau - ty to
We can - not tell Thee how much we do
E♭
3fr
B♭7
E♭
3fr
A♭
4fr
show we must a - dore Thee, if
need, Thy pre - cious pre - sence; all
B♭
E♭
3fr
A♭
4fr
B♭
Thee we would know.
sin - ners take heed.
1
E♭
3fr
2
E♭
3fr

# IRISH CAROL

Traditional Irish Carol

F F/E Dm F/C B♭ F Gm C7
3fr
both the joy - ous an - gels in strife and hur - ry fly, with
are his crown and scep - tre, where is his throne sub - lime? Where
you, O glo - rious star that with new splen - dor brings, from
mirth can ne'er con - tent us, with - out a con - science clear, and
F F/E Dm F/C B♭ Dm B♭ F
glo - ry and ho - san - nas, all Ho - ly do they cry. In
is his train ma - jes - tic that should the stars out - shine? Is
the re - mot - est parts three learn - ed east - ern kings. Turn
thus we'll find true pleas - ure in all the u - sual cheer. In
B♭ C F B♭ C
heav'n the church tri - um - phant a - dores with all her choirs, the
there no sump - tuous pal - ace, nor an - y inn at all, To
some - where else your lus - tre, your rags else - where dis - play, for
danc - ing, sport - ing, rev - 'ling with mas - quer - ade and drum, so
Dm Dm/C B♭
1 - 3 F B♭ C7 F
4 F B♭ C7 F
mil - i - tant on earth, with hum - ble faith ad - mires. But
lodge His heav'n - ly moth - er, but in a filth - y stall? O
Her - od may slay the Babe, and Christ must straight a - way. If
Christ - mas mer - ry be, as Chris - tians doth be - come.

# JESUS, THE NEWBORN BABY

Traditional Italian Carol

D7
G
is Heav - en's pre - cious Gem.
He
nes - tles Him close and warm.
"Sleep
Em
Bm
D7
is a pre - cious Gem, al - though we find Him cry - ing!
sweet - ly, my dear Son." O see him com - fort Je - sus,
G
D7
G
In Mar - y's arms He's sigh - ing,
his ti - ny Ba - by sooth - ing!
D7
G
1
2
Je - sus, our Di - a - dem.
Glo - ry to God's own Son!

# JINGLE BELLS

Words and Music by
J. PIERPONT

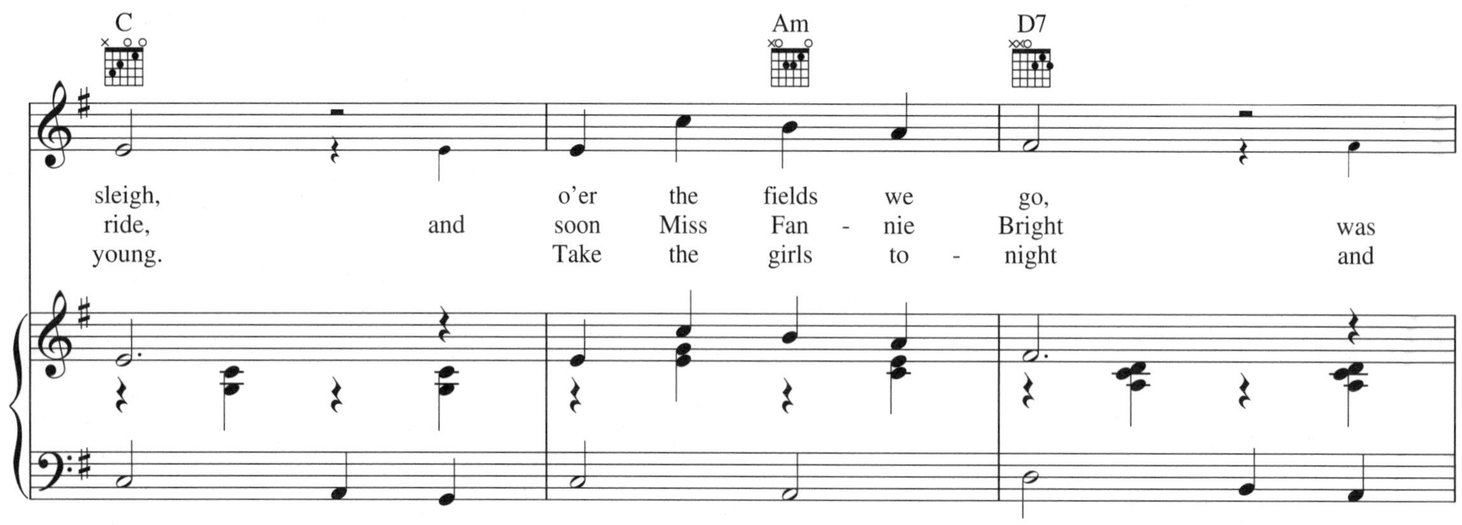

ring, mak - ing spir - its
lank, mis - for - tune seemed his
bay, two - for - ty for his
C
Am
G/D
bright; what fun it is to ride and sing a
lot; he got in - to a drift - ed bank and
speed, then hitch him to an o - pen sleigh and
D7
G
D7
G
sleigh - ing song to - night! Oh!
we, we got up - sot! Oh!
crack! you'll take the lead! Oh!
Jin - gle bells,
G7
jin - gle bells, jin - gle all the way.

C G A7

Oh, what fun it is to ride in a one - horse o - pen

D7 G

sleigh! Hey! Jin - gle bells, jin - gle bells,

G7 C

jin - gle all the way. Oh, what fun it

G D7 G

is to ride in a one - horse o - pen sleigh!

A

# LOVE CAME DOWN AT CHRISTMAS

Text by CHRISTINA ROSSETTI
Traditional Irish Melody

# JOLLY OLD ST. NICHOLAS

Traditional 19th Century American Carol

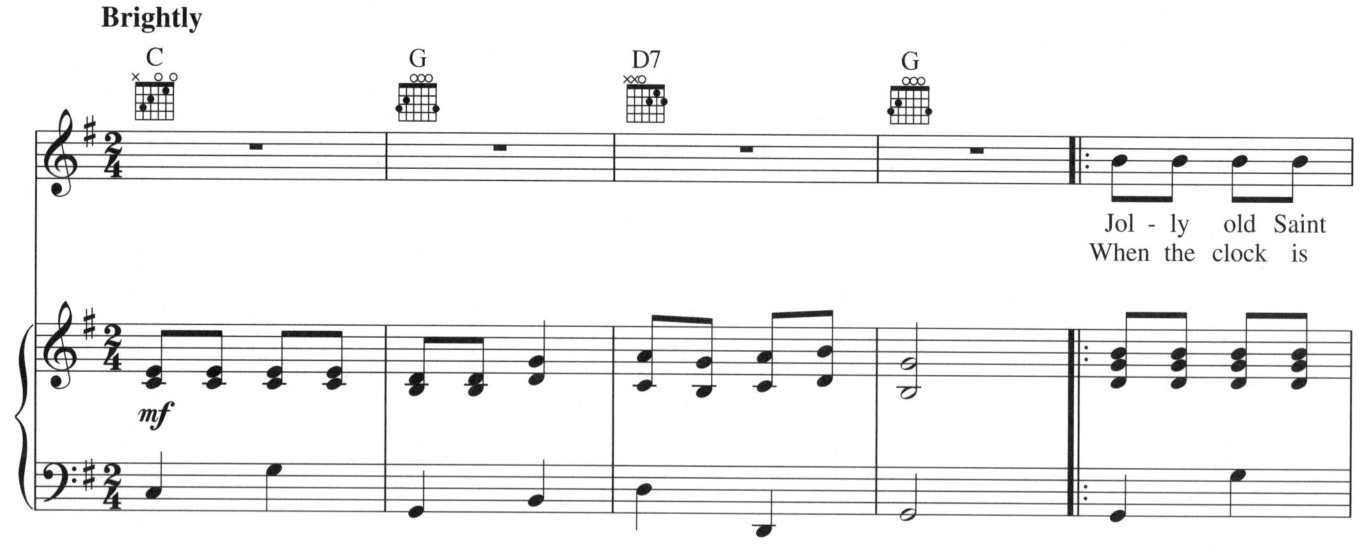


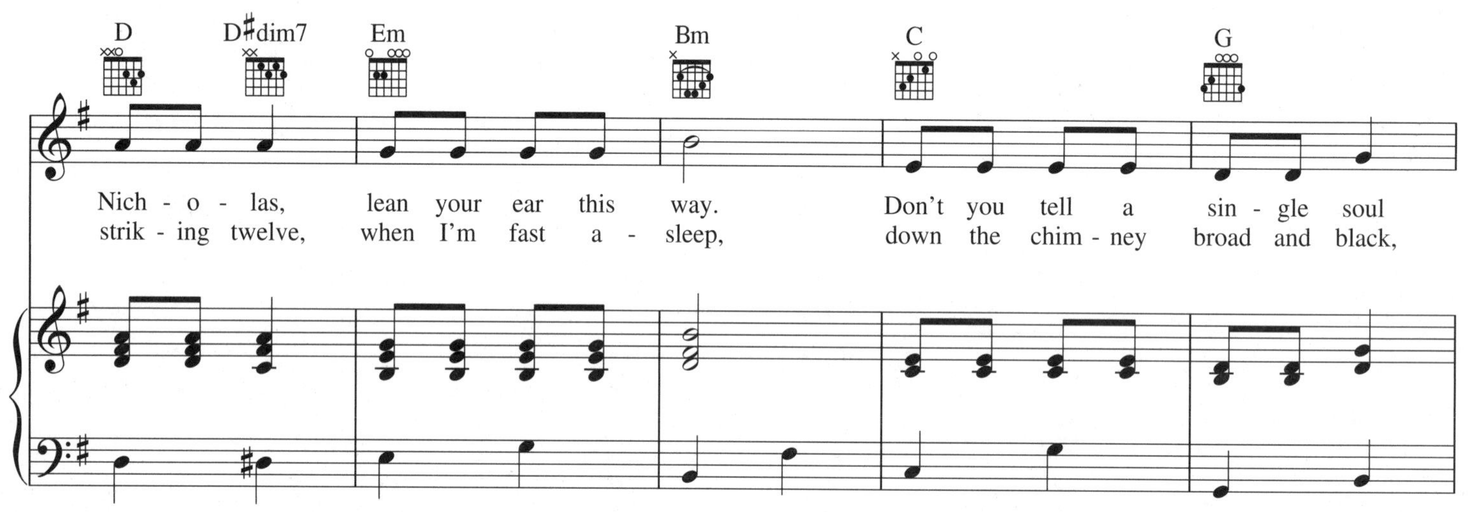


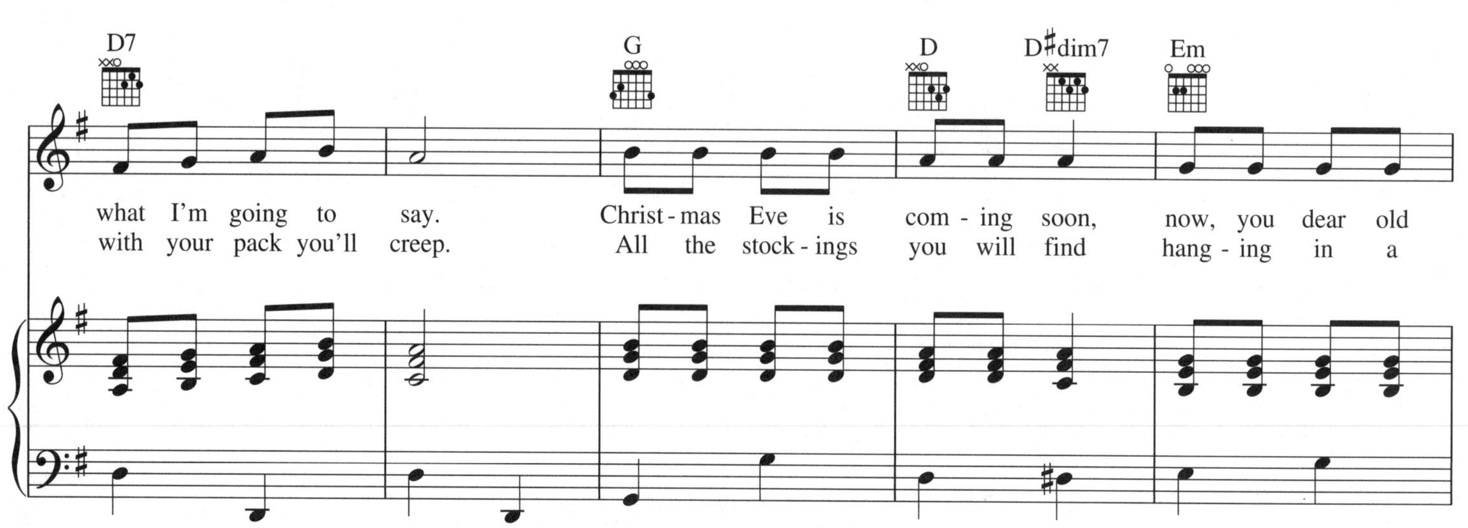

Bm
C
G
D7
1
G
2
G
man, whis - per what you'll bring to me; tell me if you can.
row. Mine will be the short - est one, you'll be sure to know.
D
D♯dim7
Em
Bm
C
John - ny wants a pair of skates; Su - sy wants a sled; Nel - lie wants a
G
D7
G
D
D♯dim7
pic - ture book, yel - low, blue and red. Now I think I'll leave to you
Em
Bm
C
G
Em
Am
D7
G
what to give the rest. Choose for me, dear San - ta Claus. You will know the best.

# JOY TO THE WORLD

Words by ISAAC WATTS
Music by GEORGE FRIDERIC HANDEL
Arranged by LOWELL MASON

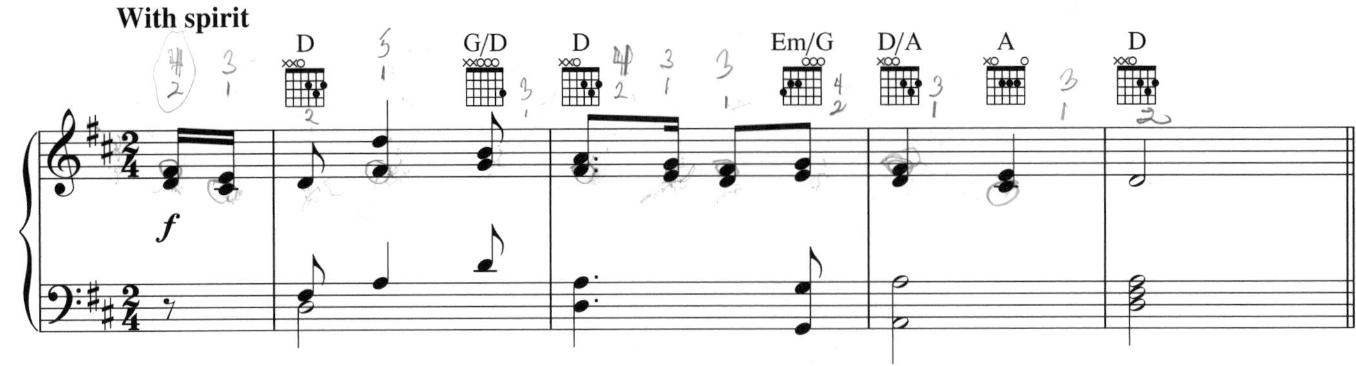


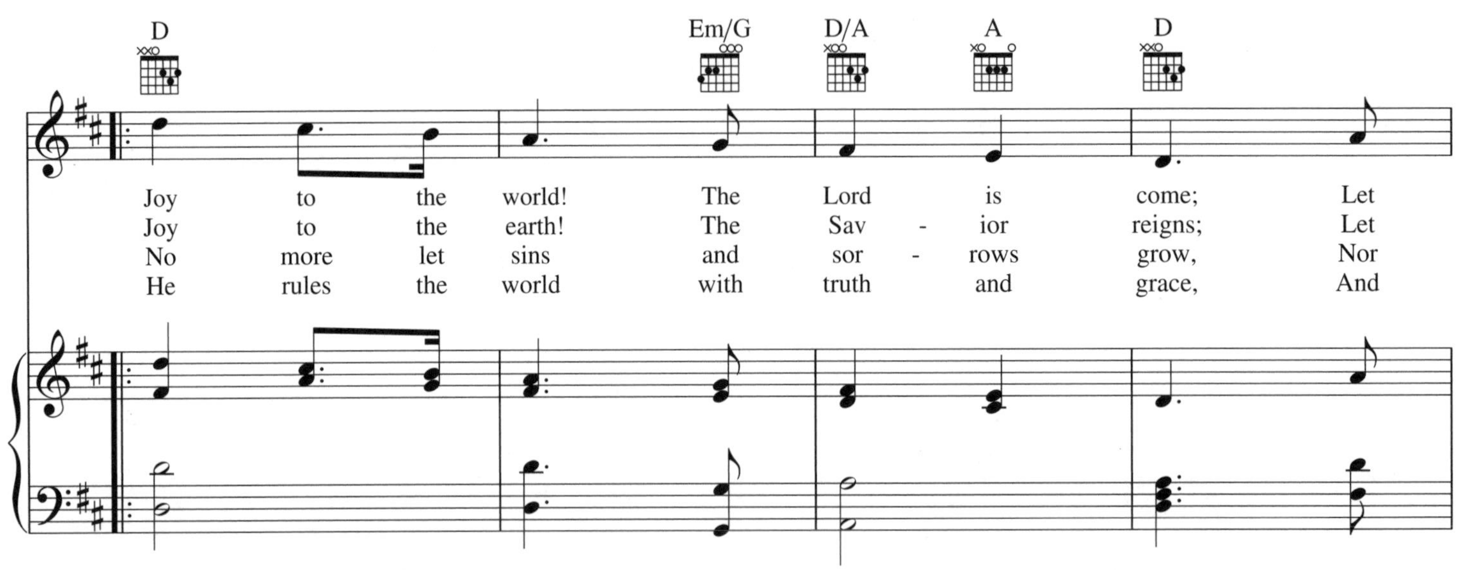


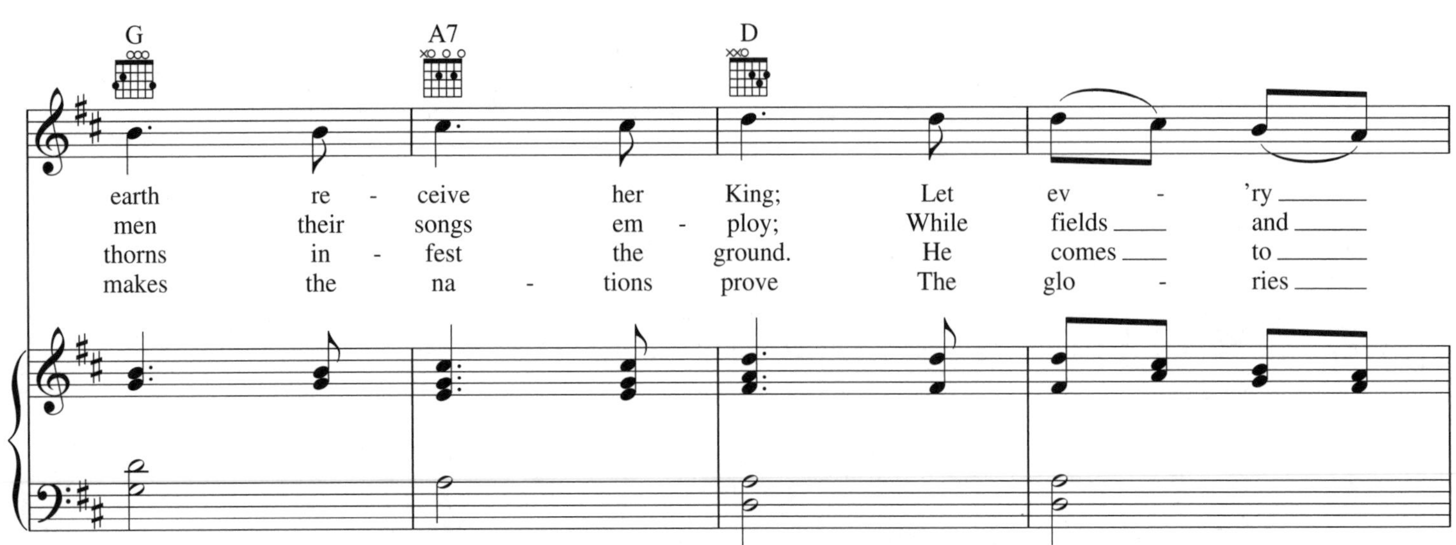

heart pre - pare Him room, and heav'n and na - ture
floods, rocks, hills and plains Re - peat the sound - ing
make His bless - ings flow Far as the curse is
of His right - eous - ness And won - ders of His

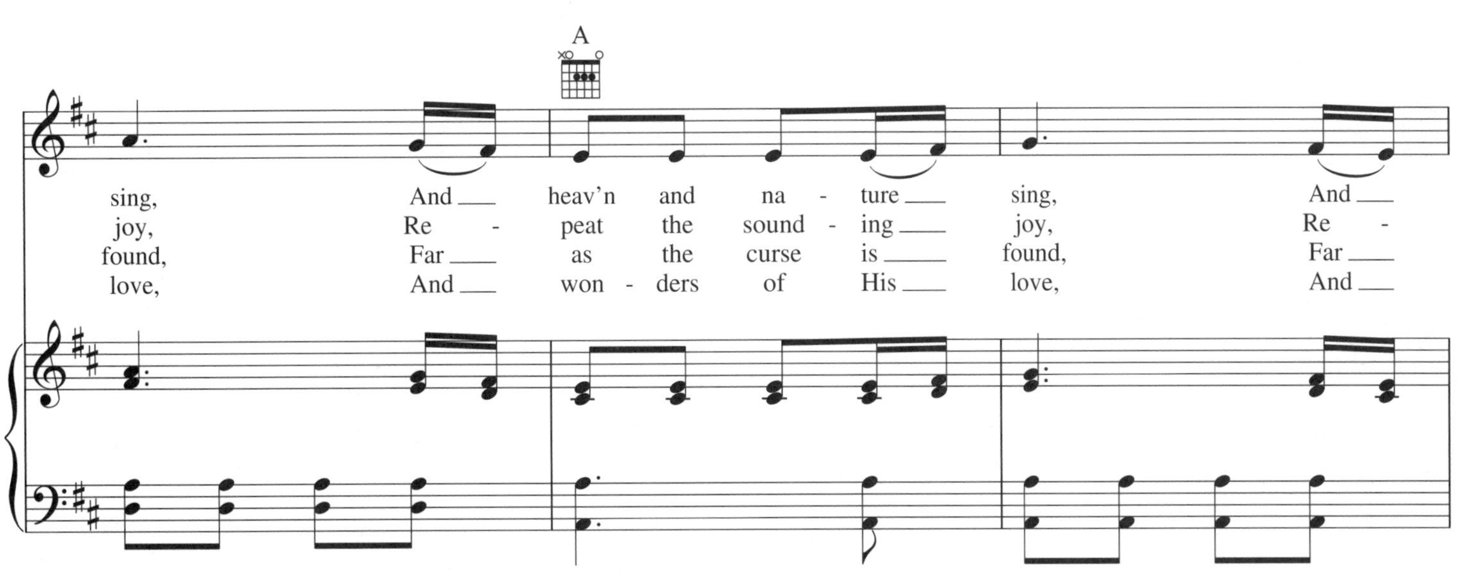
A
sing, And heav'n and na - ture sing, And
joy, Re - peat the sound - ing joy, Re -
found, Far as the curse is found, Far
love, And won - ders of His love, And

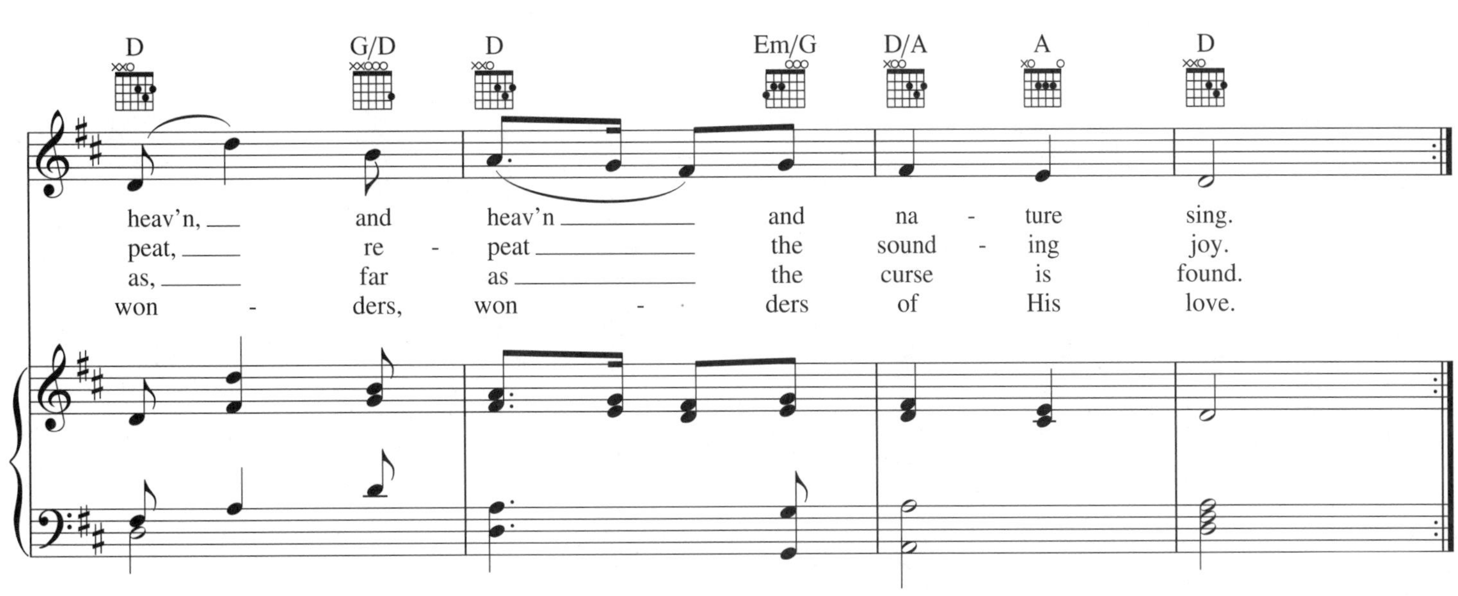
D G/D D Em/G D/A A D
heav'n, and heav'n and na - ture sing.
peat, re - peat the sound - ing joy.
as, far as the curse is found.
won - ders, won - ders of His love.

# KING HEROD

Traditional Catalonian Carol

wretch - ed King Her - od has made a de -
cross the hot des - ert to E - gypt we'll
an - gels, and birds, fly - ing down from the
D
G
D
cree, for sol - diers to kill ev - 'ry
flee, for there, dear - est Je - sus pro -
sky, the Ba - by, and Jo - seph, and
G
in - fant they see."
tect - ed will be.
Mar - y did fly.
D
1, 2
G
3
G
O
A -

# LO, HOW A ROSE E'ER BLOOMING

15th Century German Carol
Translated by THEODORE BAKER
Music from *Alte Catholische Geistliche Kirchengesäng*

E Am D7/A G/B Am D7 G/D D7sus D7 G C G D
ter, When half spent was the night. I - sa - iah 'twas fore - told
Em C G/D D Am/E Em G/D D7 G C G D
it, The Rose I have in mind, With Mar - y we be - hold
Em C G/D D Am/E Em G/D D7 G Am Bm Em/G A D
it, The Vir - gin Moth - er kind. To show God's love a - right,
D7/F♯ G C G D E Am D7/A G/B Am/C D7 G/D D7sus D7 G
She bore to men a Sav - ior, When half spent was the night.

# LULLABY, JESUS

Traditional Polish Carol

B♭
C7
Lul - la by, Je - sus, O sleep now, my
F
C7/E
F
pre - cious, Moth - er is watch - ing with
C
F
love none can meas - ure.
C7/E
F
C
F

# MARCH OF THE THREE KINGS

Words by M.L. HOHMAN
Traditional French Melody

Cm Gm Cm D7 Cm7 D7 Gm D7 Cm/E♭ D7
Fine
Kings of East with all their fine ar - ray. The gifts of
Cm7 D7 Cm/E♭ D7♯5 Cm D7♯5 Cm/E♭ Gm/D C♯dim
gold, frank - in - cense and myrrh were guard - ed close by a
Cm C♯dim D7 Cm/E♭ D7 Cm7 D7 Cm/E♭ D7♯5
band of stur - dy war - riors, their swords, their shields, and their buck - lers
Cm7 D7♯5 Cm/E♭ Gm/D Cm D7 E♭6 Edim F9sus D7 Gm
D.S. al Fine
bright, a gleam and spar - kling in the morn - ing light.

# MARY HAD A BABY

African-American Spiritual

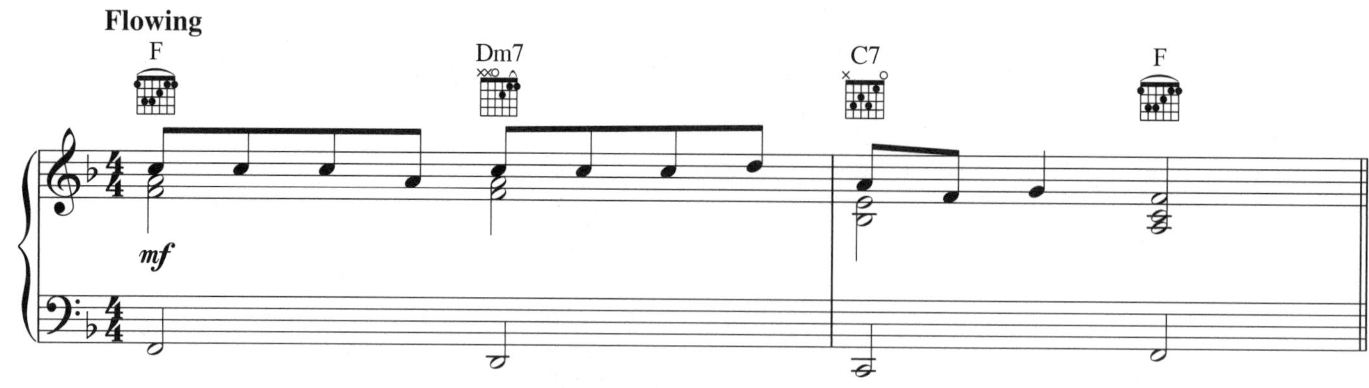

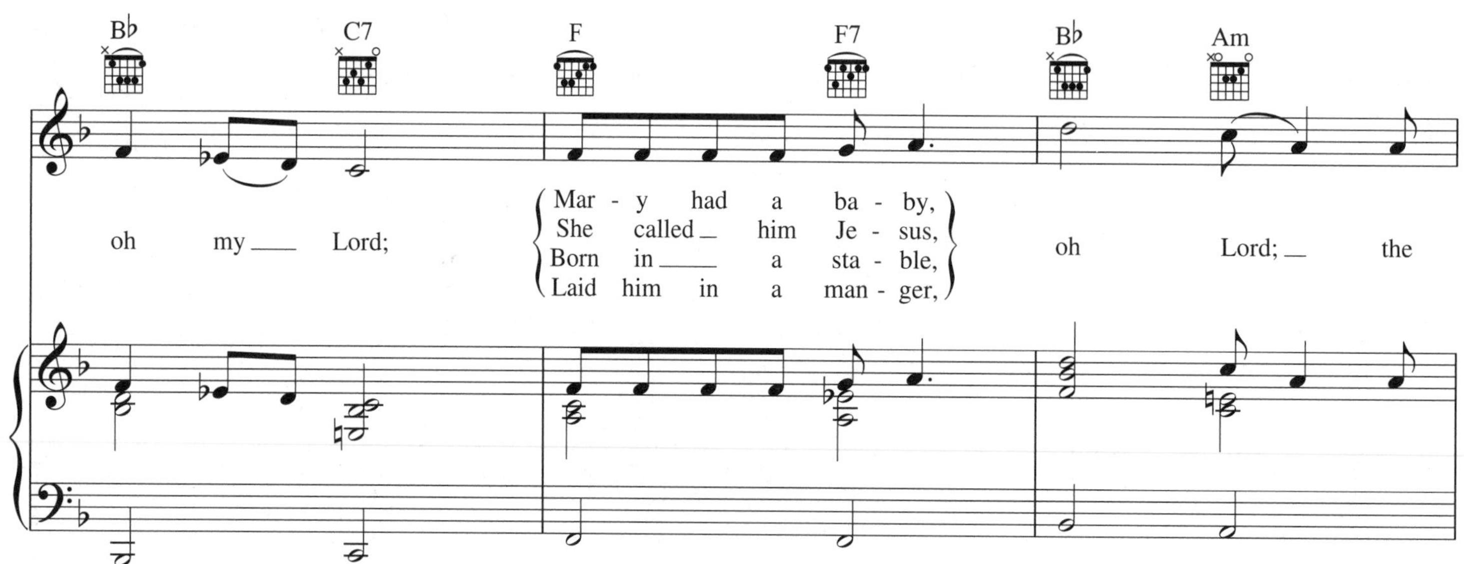

F
Dm7
C7
F
Dm7
people keep a-coming and the train done gone.
C7
F
B♭
F
What did she name Him?
Where was He born?
Where did they lay Him?
Mary had a baby.
Oh Lord;
B♭
C7
F
F7
What did she name Him?
Where was He born?
Where did they lay Him?
Mary had a baby.
Oh my Lord;
What did she name Him?
Where was He born?
Where did they lay Him?
Mary had a baby.
B♭
Am
F
Dm7
C7
F
Oh Lord; the people keep a-coming and the train done gone.

# MASTERS IN THIS HALL

Traditional English

Dm
Em7♭5
Dm/F
A/G
No - ël! No - ël! No - ël! No - ël! sing we
No - ël! No - ël! No - ël! No - ël! sing we
Dm/F
D7/F♯
Gm
clear! Hol - pen are all folk on earth Born
loud! God to - day hath all folk raised And
Dm/F
A7
Dm
is God's Son, so dear.
cast a - down the proud.
A7/E
Gm/B♭
This is Christ, the Lord; Mas - ters, be ye glad!

Dm A7/E Dm/F Gm/B♭ A7 Dm

Christ - mas is come in and no folk shall be sad:

Dm Em7♭5 Dm/F A/G Dm Em7♭5

No - ël! No - ël! No - ël! No - ël! sing we
No - ël! No - ël! No - ël! No - ël! sing we

Dm/F D7/F♯ Gm A/G Dm/F Gm

clear! Hol - pen are all folk on earth Born
loud! God to - day hath all folk raised And

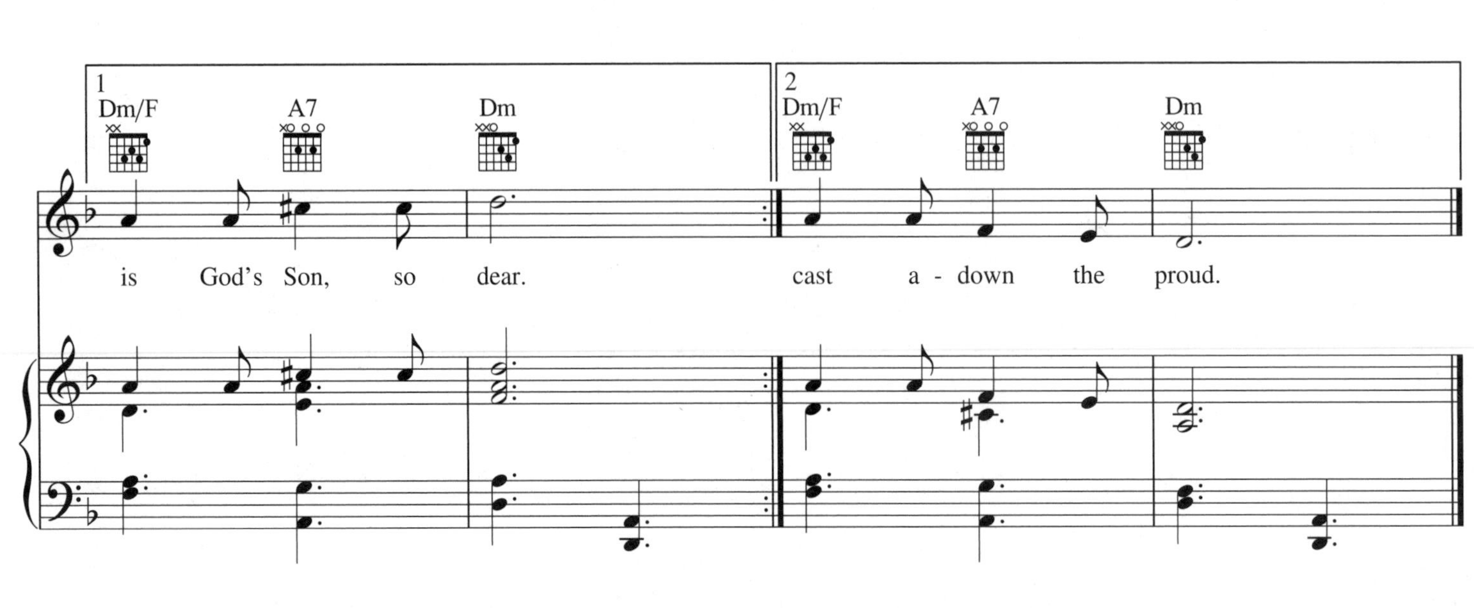

# O COME, O COME, IMMANUEL

Plainsong, 13th Century
Words translated by JOHN M. NEALE
and HENRY S. COFFIN

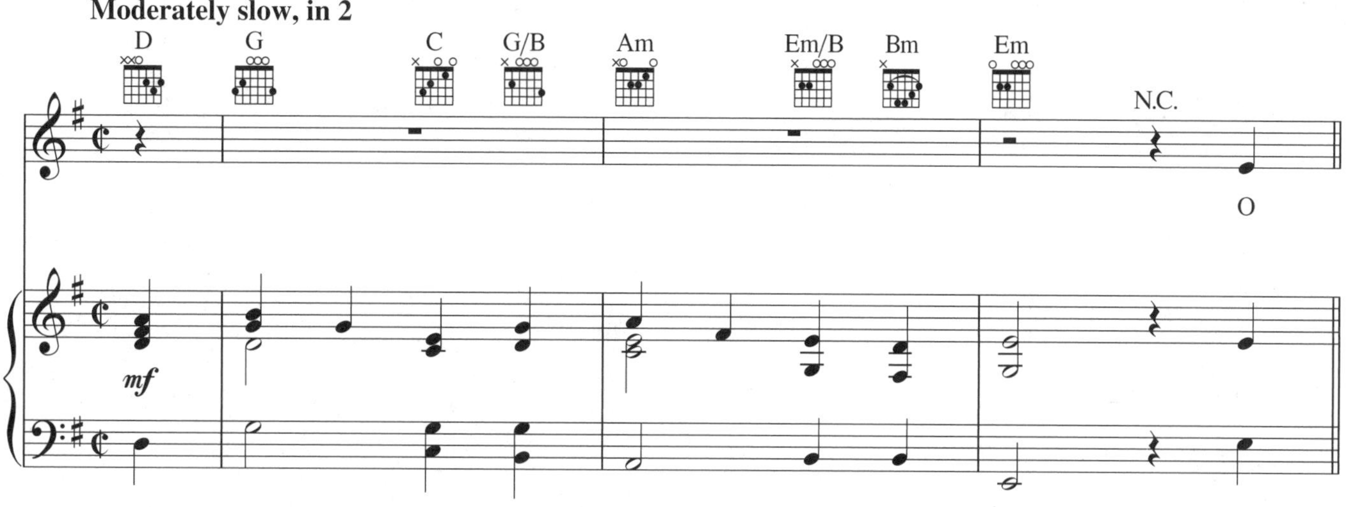


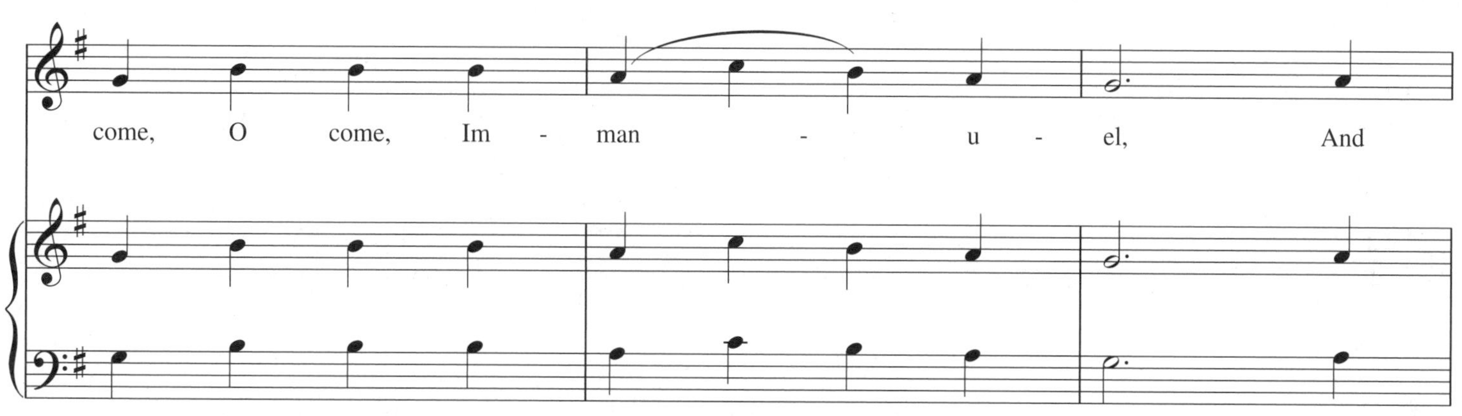

ex - ile here Un - til the Son of God ap -
G D Em Bm G C D
pear. Re - joice, re - joice! Im - man - u -
Em D G C G/B Am Em/B Bm Em
el shall come to Thee, O Is - ra - el! O
Am Em G C
come, Thou key of Da - vid, come, And o - pen wide our

Am
Em
Bm
Em
Am
Em/B
Bm
Em
D/A
A7
heav'n - ly home. Make safe the way that leads on
D
Em
D
Bm
G
Am
G/D
D7
high And close the path to mis - er -
G
D
Em
Bm
G
C
D
y. Re - joice, re - joice! Im - man - u -
Em
D
G
C
G/B
Am
Em/B
Bm
Em
el shall come to Thee, O Is - ra - el!

# NOËL NOUVELET

Traditional French Carol

D
Gm
3fr
Sing we No - ël for Christ the new - born
King, No - ël. Christ - mas comes a - gain, oh,
C
1, 2
sing we all No - ël.
3
ël.

# O BETHLEHEM

Traditional Spanish

E♭dim7
F7
B♭7
B♭/A♭
Cm/G
G/F
an - gels bring to ___ the
Cm
B♭7/D
A♭/E♭
B♭7/D
B♭7
A♭/C
C♯dim7
world glad news of an in - fant King; Round you the
Dm7♭5
G7
Cm
E♭/B♭
B♭/A♭
hills and val - leys are ech - o - ing!
E♭/G
Fm6
B♭7
E♭
B♭7
E♭
O Beth - le - hem, ___ O Beth - le - hem.

# O CHRISTMAS TREE

Traditional German Carol

Fmaj7
D7♭5(♭9)
D9
Gm
Gm7
C9
boughs are green in sum - mer's glow, and do not fade in
ev - 'ry year the Christ - mas tree brings to us all both
bough doth hold its ti - ny light that makes each toy to
B♭dim7/F
F
B♭/C
C/B♭
A
D7
win - ter's snow. O Christ - mas tree, O Christ - mas tree, you
joy and glee. O Christ - mas tree, O Christ - mas tree, much
spar - kle bright. O Christ - mas tree, O Christ - mas tree, thy
Gm
D
Gm
C7
1, 2
B♭dim7/F
F
3
B♭dim7/F
F
stand in ver - dant beau - ty! O
pleas - ure doth thou bring me! O
can - dles shine out bright - ly! O
F/E
Cm6/E♭
D7sus
D7
Gm
D
Gm
C7
Fsus
F
Christ - mas tree, O Christ - mas tree, thy can - dles shine out bright - ly!

# O COME, ALL YE FAITHFUL
## (Adeste fideles)

Music by JOHN FRANCIS WADE
Latin Words translated by FREDERICK OAKELEY

G
D7
G
D7sus
D7
G
D
G
Em
Am
Come and be - hold Him, born the King of
Glo - ry to God in the
Word of the Fa - ther, now in flesh ap -
D
G
D
G
D7
G
an - gels.
high - est.
pear - ing.
O come, let us a - dore Him, O
D
G
D7
G
D
G
D7
G
D
A7
come, let us a - dore Him, O come, let us a -
D
G
C
G/D
D7
G
dore Him, Christ, the Lord!

# O COME, LITTLE CHILDREN

Words by C. VON SCHMIDT
Music by J.P.A. SCHULZ

B♭
E♭
B♭7
E♭
poor and so hum - ble, so sweet and so mild. Now "Glo - ry to
B♭7
E♭
God!" sing the an - gels on high, And "Peace up - on earth!" heav'n - ly
B♭7
E♭
B♭
B♭7
E♭
voic - es re - ply. Then come, lit - tle chil - dren, and join in the
A♭
B♭
E♭
B♭7
E♭
day That glad - dened the world on that first Christ-mas Day.

# O HOLY NIGHT

French Words by PLACIDE CAPPEAU
English Words by JOHN S. DWIGHT
Music by ADOLPHE ADAM

C/E F C C7
world in sin and er - ror pin - ing, till He ap -
break, for the slave is our broth - er, and in His
Em/B B7 Em
peared and the soul felt its worth. A
name all op - pres - sion shall cease. Sweet
G7 C
thrill of hope the wea - ry world re - joic - es, for
hymns of joy in grate - ful cho - rus raise we, let
G7 C
yon - der breaks a new and glo - rious morn.
all with - in us praise His ho - ly name.

Am
Em
Fall on your knees, oh,
Christ is the Lord, oh,
Dm
Am
hear the an - gel voic - es! O
praise His name for - ev - er! His
C
G/F
C/E
F
night di - vine, O
pow'r and glo - ry
C/G
G7
C
night when Christ was born! O
ev - er - more pro - claim! His
cresc.

1
G
G/F
C/E
F
night di - vine, O
C/G
G7
C
night, O night di - vine!
decresc.
2
G
G/F
C/E
F
pow'r and glo - ry
C/G
G7
C
ev - er - more pro - claim!
decresc.
rit.

# O LITTLE TOWN OF BETHLEHEM

Words by PHILLIPS BROOKS
Music by LEWIS H. REDNER

*Additional Lyrics*

3. How silently, how silently
The wondrous Gift is giv'n!
So God imparts to human hearts
The blessings of His heav'n.
No ear may hear His coming,
But in this world of sin,
Where meek souls will receive Him still,
The dear Christ enters in.

4. O Holy Child of Bethlehem,
Descend to us, we pray.
Cast out our sin, and enter in,
Be born in us today.
We hear the Christmas angels
The great glad tidings tell.
O come to us, abide with us,
Our Lord Immanuel!

# O SANCTISSIMA

Sicilian Carol

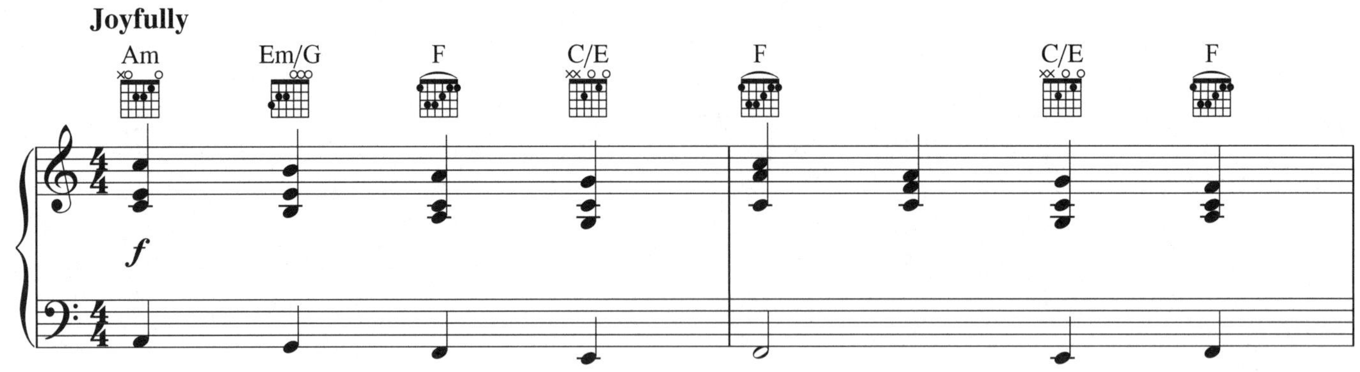


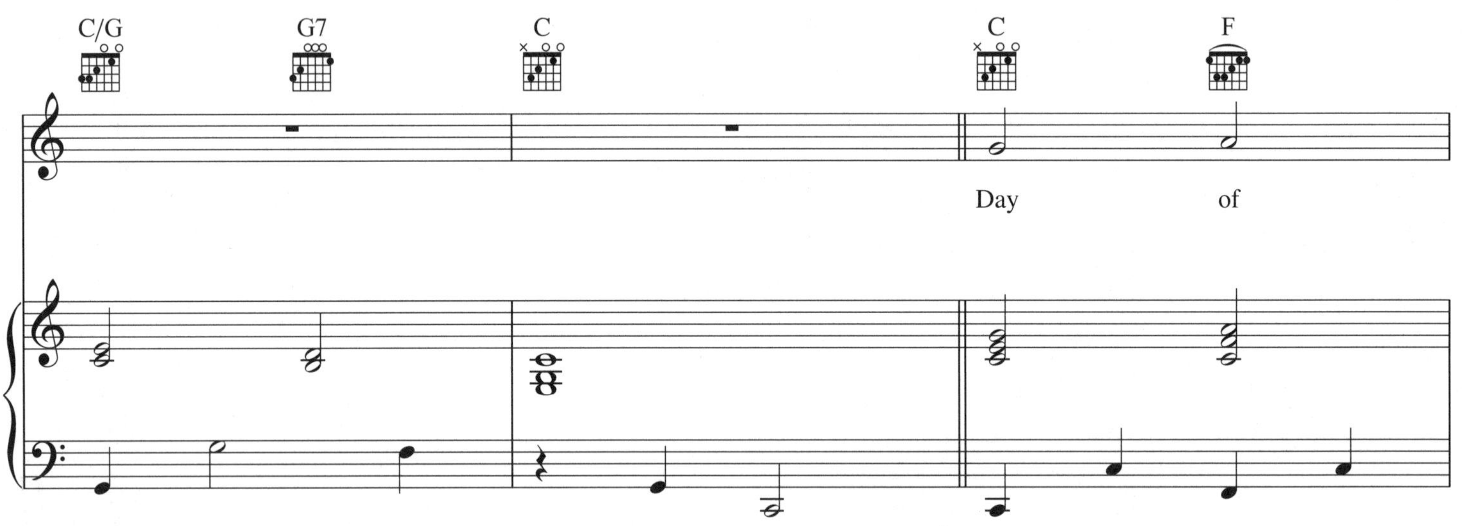


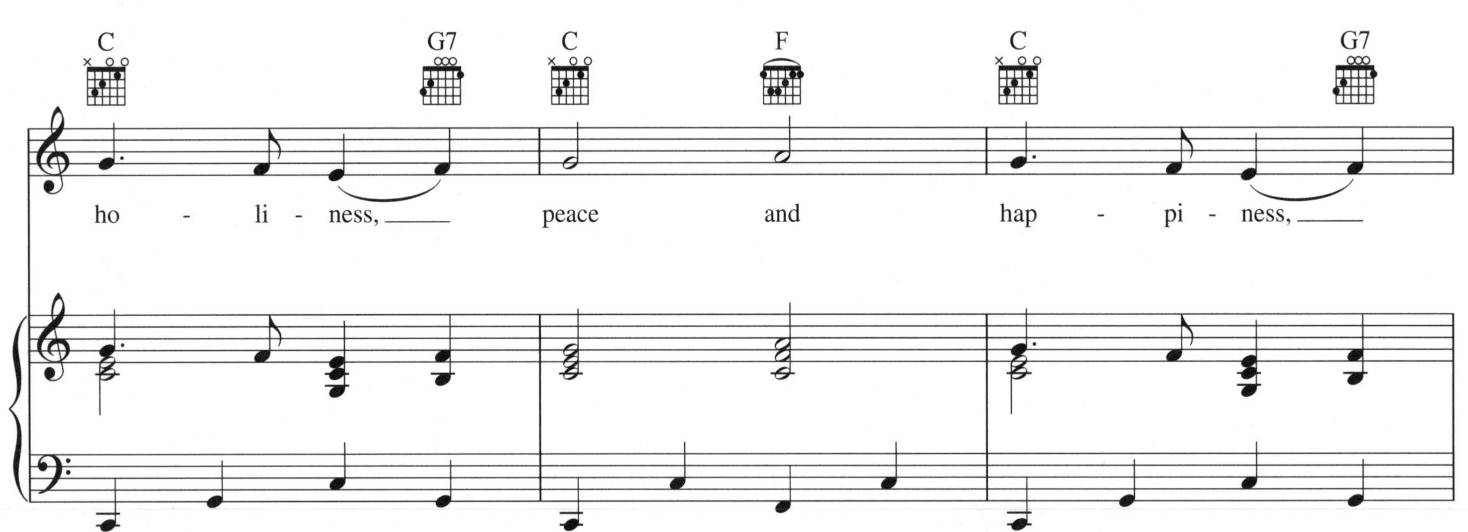

C G/B D/A G C/E G/D D7
Joy - ful, glo - ri - ous Christ - mas
G G7
day! An - gels tell the sto - ry
C Am Em/G F C/E
of this day of glo - ry, Praise Christ, our
F C/E F C/G G7 C
Sav - ior, born this Christ - mas day!

# PASTORES A BELEN

Traditional Puerto Rican Carol

C
G
D
come, O come, O Shep - herds, run to
G
C
G
see, the Ho - ly Child, that
D
G
brings us Heav - en's peace. Come car - ry - ing some
D
G
nuts and some hon - ey, of - fer them to Je - sus to eat, come

D
car - ry - ing some nuts and some hon - ey, of - fer them to
G
D
G
Je - sus to eat. Has - ten, has - ten, haste to a - dore!
D
G
D
Je - sus is born, the Son of our great Lord, Je - sus our King, for -
G
D
G
ev - er - more.

# O THOU JOYFUL

Traditional German Carol

# OH! INFANT JESUS

Traditional Italian Carol

G
D
G
D
Am
dwell there - in. So I will nev - er - more
hum - bly pray while I kneel and mar - vel
G
D
G
be dis - tressed.
at Your birth.
With hearts that o - ver -
D
C
Am
G
C
B
Em
flow with love, we wor - ship Thee, King of
G/D
D7
1
G
2
G
Heav'n a - bove. bove.

# ONCE IN ROYAL DAVID'S CITY

Words by CECIL F. ALEXANDER
Music by HENRY J. GAUNTLETT

C/G G Am7 D7/F# G C/G G D7 G
Mar - y was that moth - er mild. Je - sus Christ her lit - tle Child.
D7/G G D7/G G Em/G Bm D7 G
And our eyes at last shall see Him Through His own re - deem - ing love,
D7/G G D7/G G Em/G Bm D7 G
For that Child so dear and gen - tle Is our Lord in heav'n a - bove;
C/G G Am/G D7/F# G C/G G D7 G
And He leads His chil - dren on To the place where He is gone.

# PAT-A-PAN
## (Willie, Take Your Little Drum)

Words and Music by
BERNARD de la MONNOYE

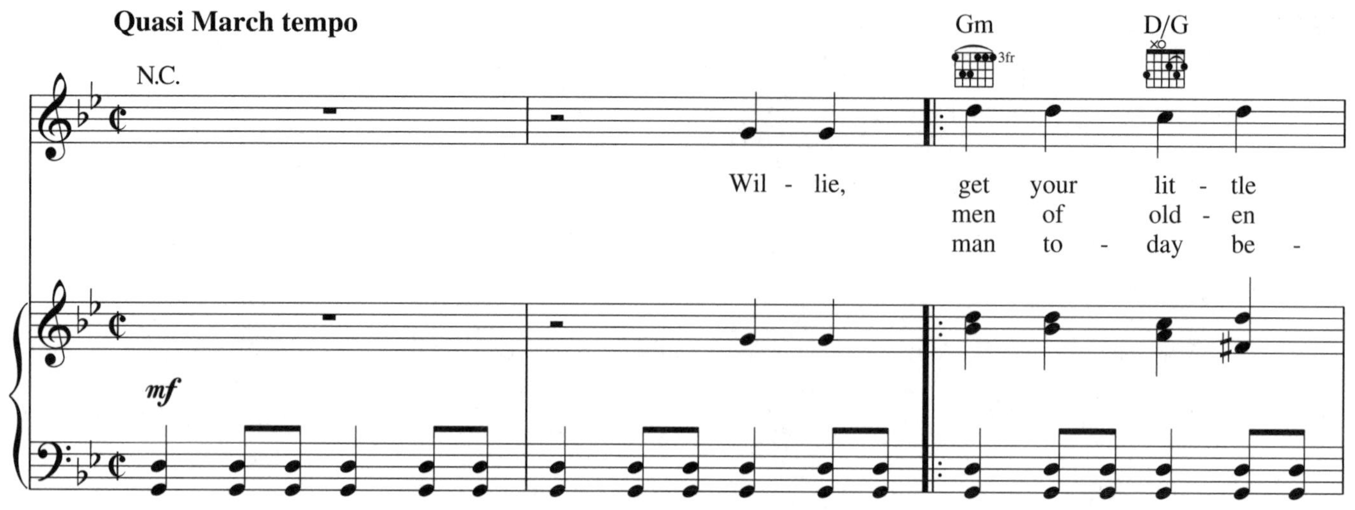

Cm6/G
D7/G
Gm
Cm/G
3fr
When you play your fife and drum, How can an - y -
pan. And al - so the drums they'd play Full of joy, on
As the in - stru - ments you play, We will sing this

1, 2
Gm
Cm6/G
Gm
3fr
one be glum? When the
Christ - mas day. God and
Christ - mas

3
Gm
3fr
day.

# REJOICE AND BE MERRY

Traditional English Carol

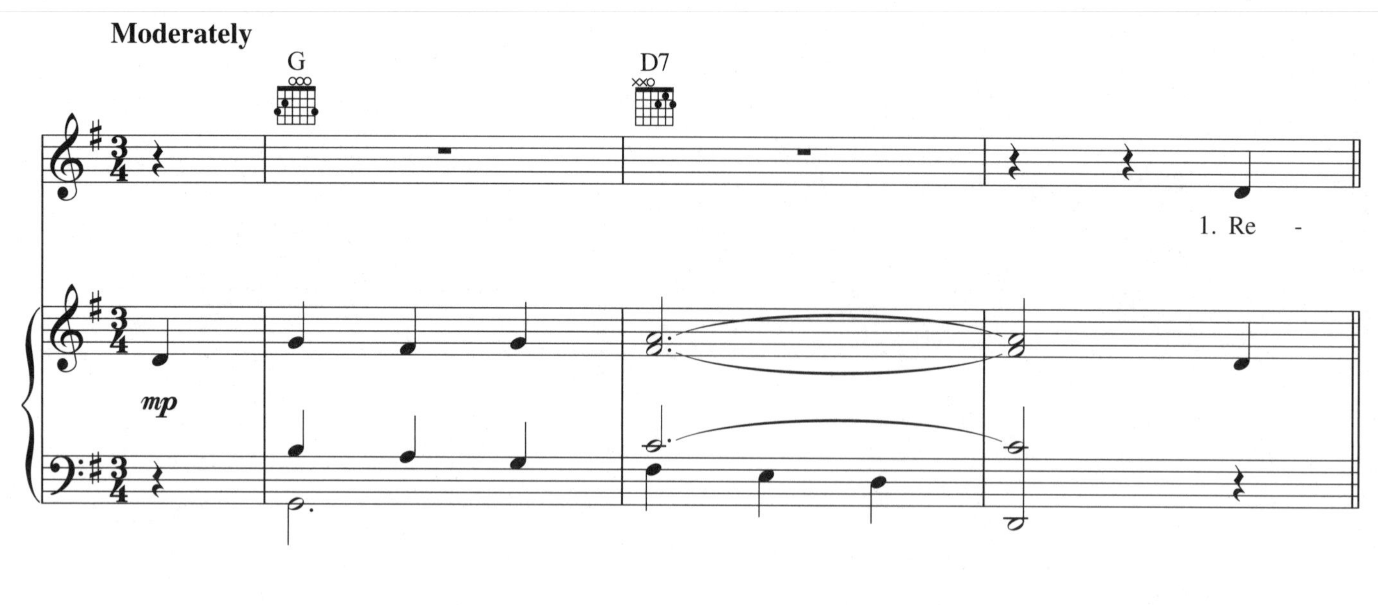


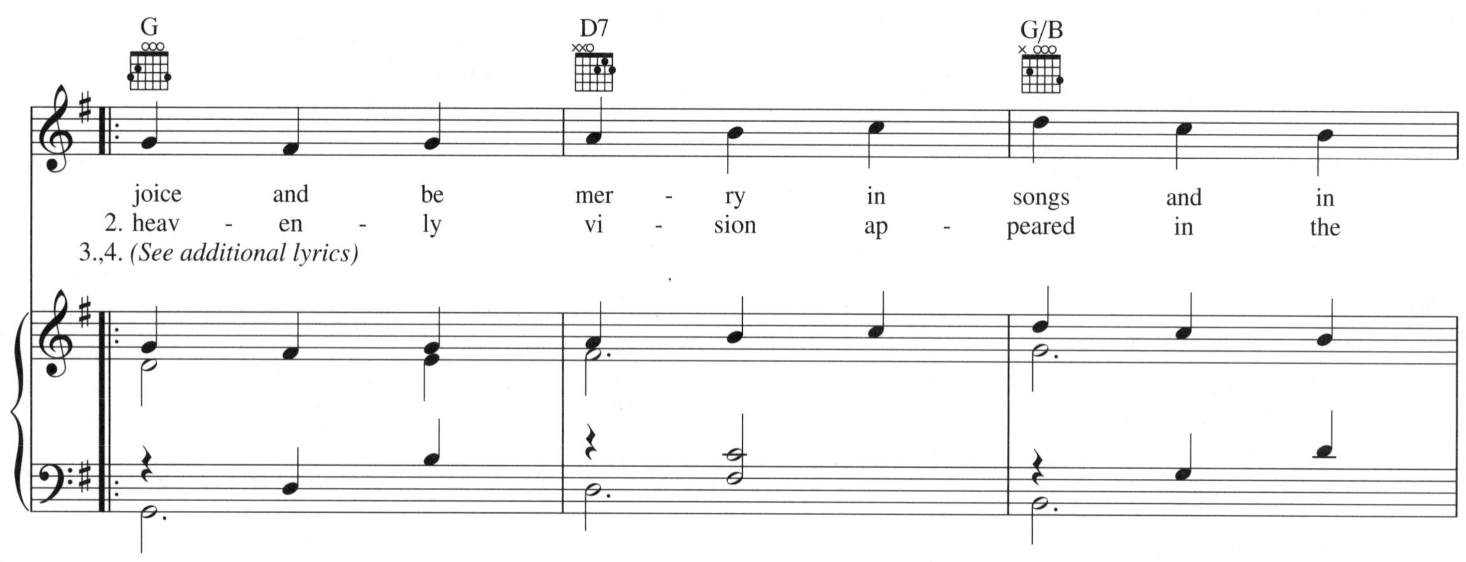


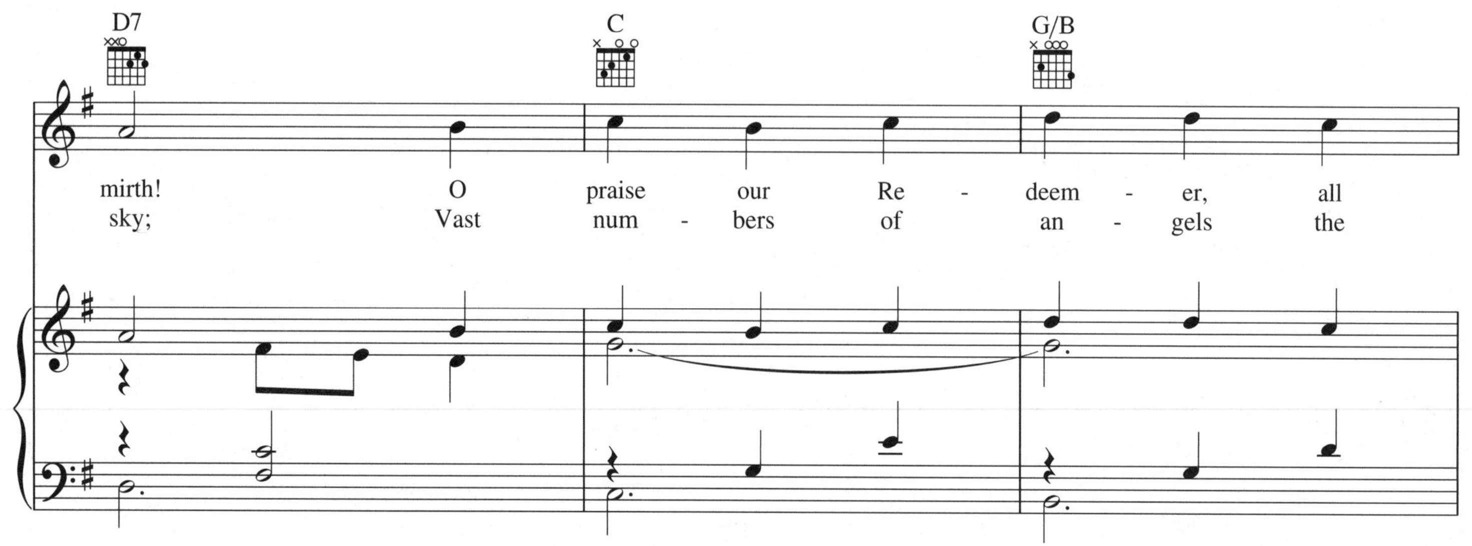

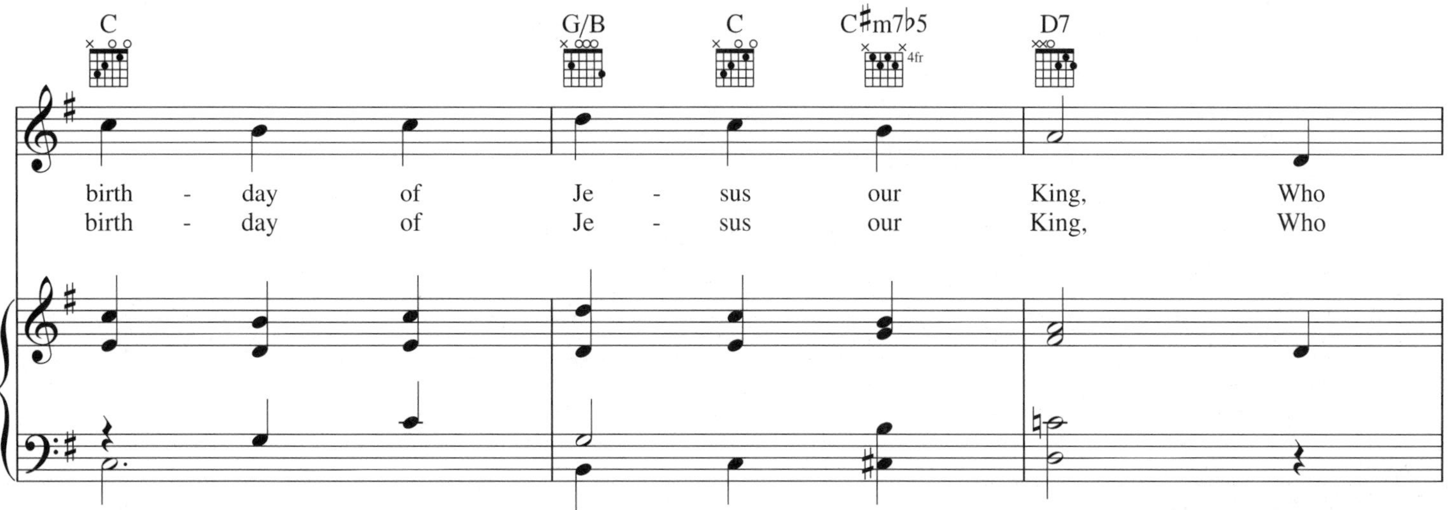


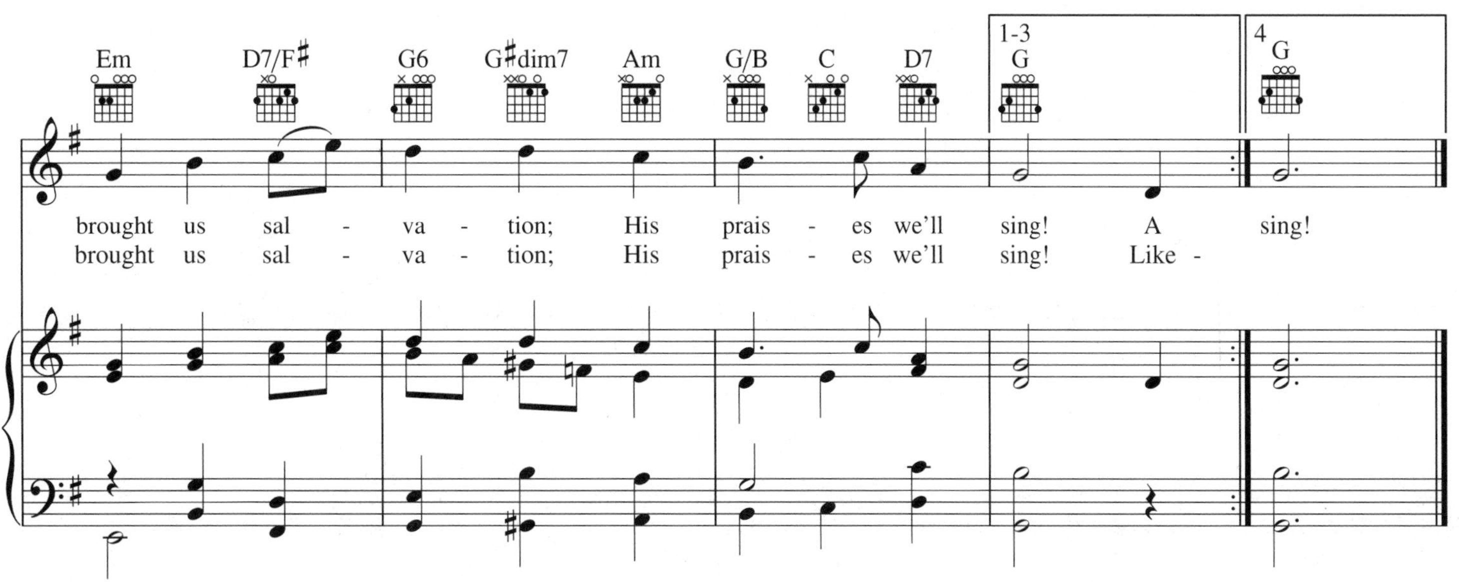


*Additional Lyrics*

3. Likewise a bright star in the sky did appear,
Which led the wise men from the east to draw near.
They found the Messiah, sweet Jesus our King,
Who brought us salvation; His praises we'll sing!

4. And when they were come, they their treasures unfold,
And unto Him offered myrrh, incense and gold.
So blessed forever be Jesus our King,
Who brought us salvation; His praises we'll sing!

# RING OUT, YE WILD AND MERRY BELLS

Words and Music by
C. MAITLAND

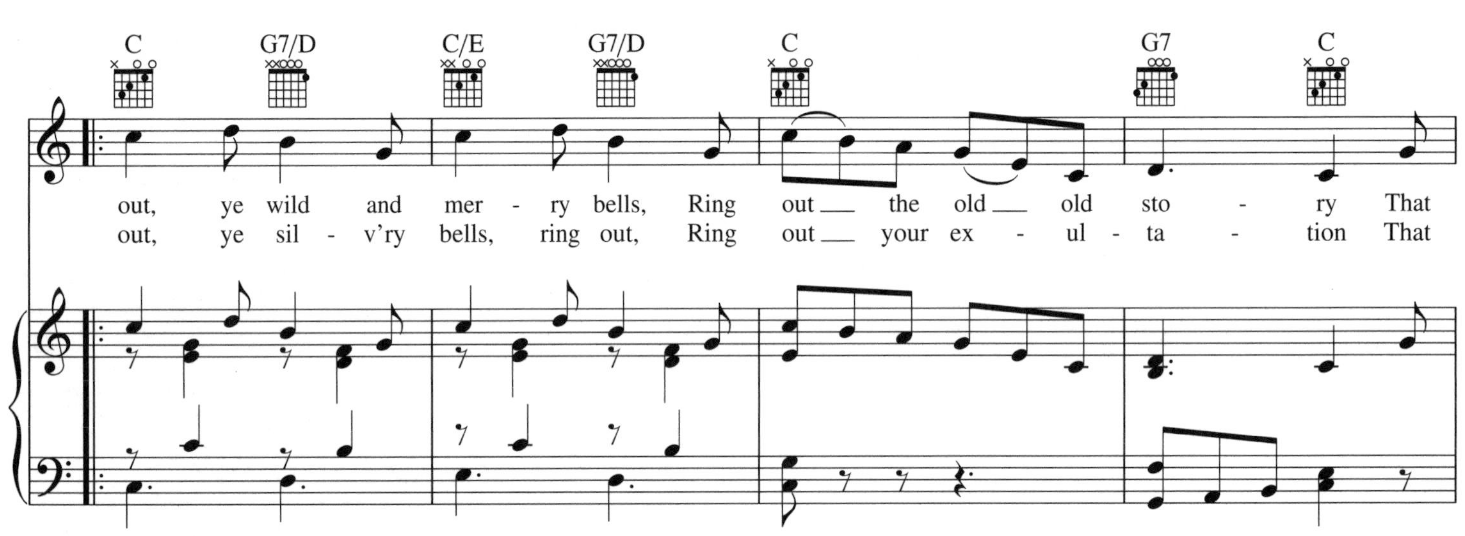


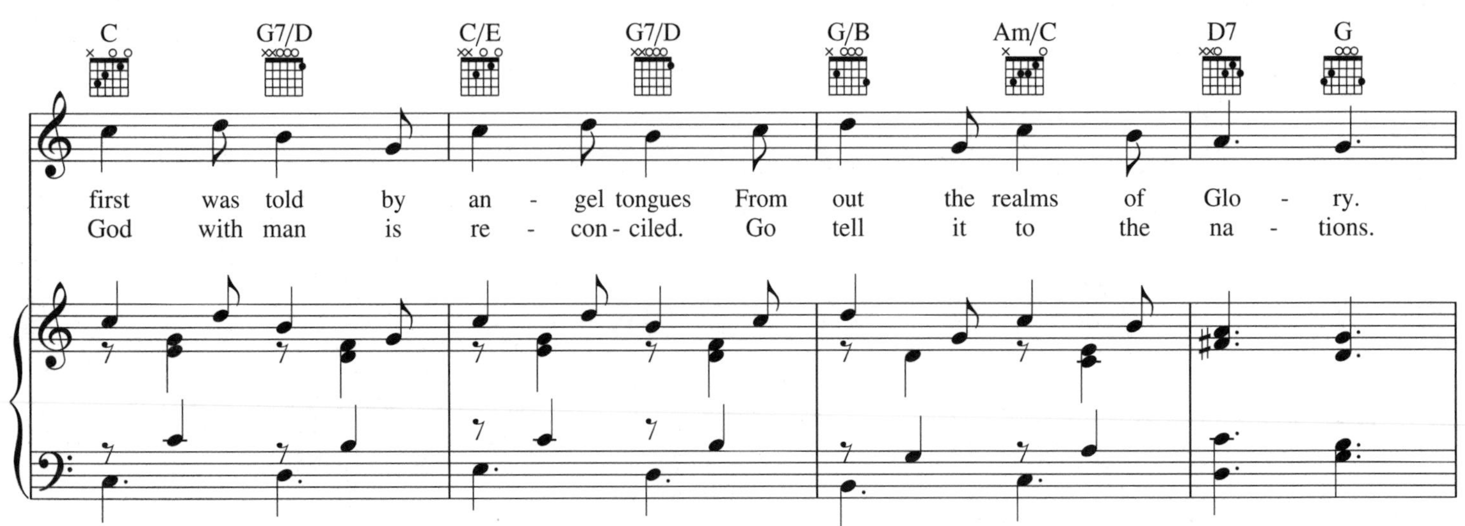

Em
D7 G7 C7 F A7/E
Peace on earth was their sweet song, Glo - ry in the high - est! Ech - o - ing all the
There - fore let us all to - day, Glo - ry in the high - est! Ban - ish sor - row
D7 G7 E7 Am7 D7 G7 C F/C
hills a - way, Glo - ry in the high - est!
far a - way, Glo - ry in the high - est!
Ring, sweet bells, ring
C7 F/C F C7/F F D7/F♯ G/F
ev - er - more, Peal from ev - 'ry stee - ple. Christ, the Lord, shall
E7 Am F♯dim7 C Am7
1, 2
G7 C
3
G7 C
be our God And we shall be His peo - ple! Ring peo - ple!

# RING, LITTLE BELLS

Words by KARL ENSLIN
Traditional German Carol

G7
C
F
G7
Do not block the door - way on my bless - ed
To us shel - ter giv - ing and the Child
joy and bless - ing ho - ly from the Child so
C
F
birth - day!
prais - ing?
low - ly.
Ring, bells, go ding - a - ling - a - ling.
C
F
1, 2
Ring, lit - tle bells!
3
B♭
C
F

# ROCKING

Traditional Czech Carol

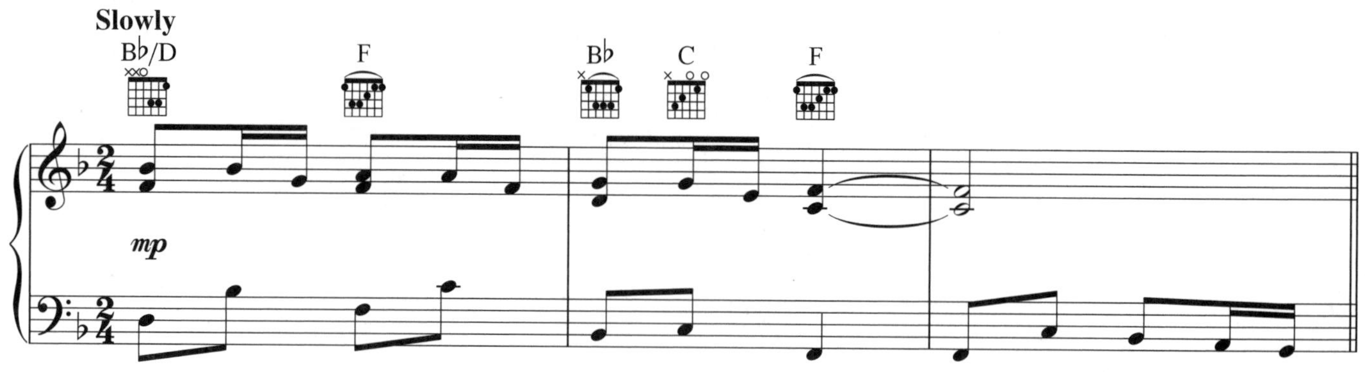

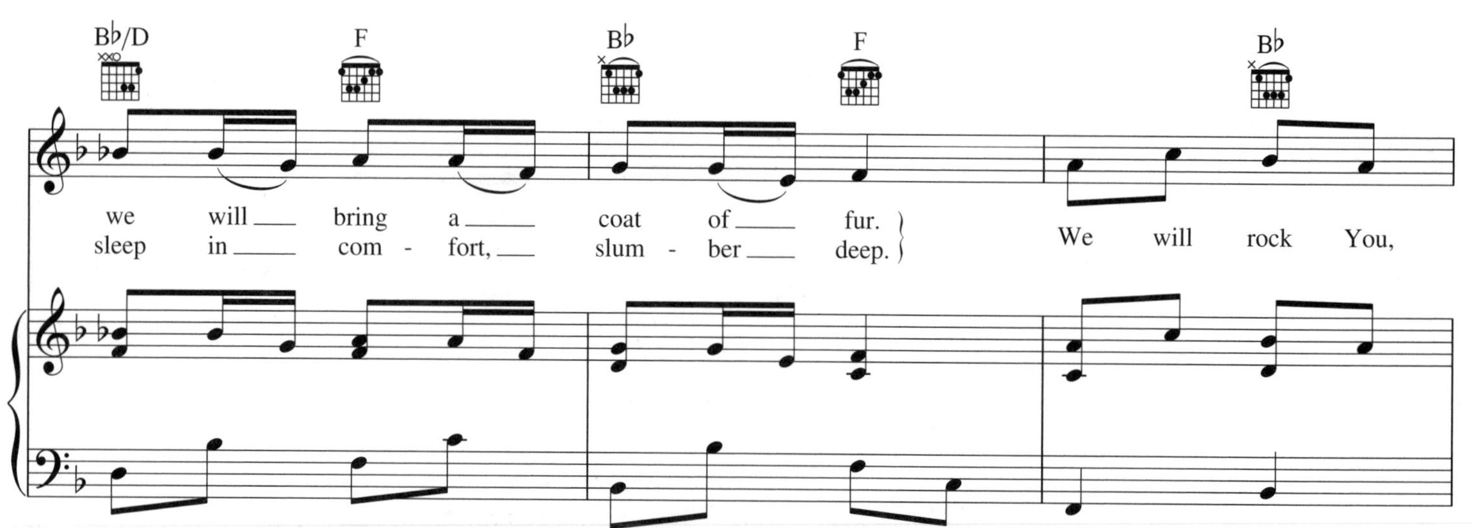

C
F
B♭
C
rock You, rock You. Gent - ly slum - ber as we rock You.
F
G
C
See the fur to keep You warm,
We will praise You all we can,
B♭/D
F
B♭
C
F
B♭
F
snug - ly fits Your ti - ny form.
dar - ling, dar - ling lit - tle man.
1
C
F
2
C
F

# SILENT NIGHT

Words by JOSEPH MOHR
Translated by JOHN F. YOUNG
Music by FRANZ X. GRUBER

B♭
E♭
3fr
Moth - er and Child. Ho - ly In - fant so
heav - en a - far, Heav'n - ly hosts sing
Thy ho - ly face With the dawn of re -
B♭
F7
ten - der and mild, Sleep in heav - en - ly
Al - le - lu - ia, Christ the Sav - ior is
deem - ing grace, Je - sus, Lord, at Thy
B♭
B♭/F
F7
peace, Sleep in heav - en - ly
born! Christ the Sav - ior is
birth. Je - sus, Lord, at Thy
1, 2
B♭
3
B♭
peace.
born!
birth.

# THE SIMPLE BIRTH

Traditional Flemish Carol

*Additional Lyrics*

3. His eyes of blackest jet were sparkling with light, *(Repeat)*
   Rosy cheeks bloomed on His face fair and bright. *(Repeat)*

4. And from His lovely mouth, the laughter did swell, *(Repeat)*
   When He saw Mary, whom He loved so well. *(Repeat)*

5. He came to weary earth, so dark and so drear, *(Repeat)*
   To wish mankind a blessed New Year. *(Repeat)*

# SING WE NOW OF CHRISTMAS
## (Noël nouvelet)

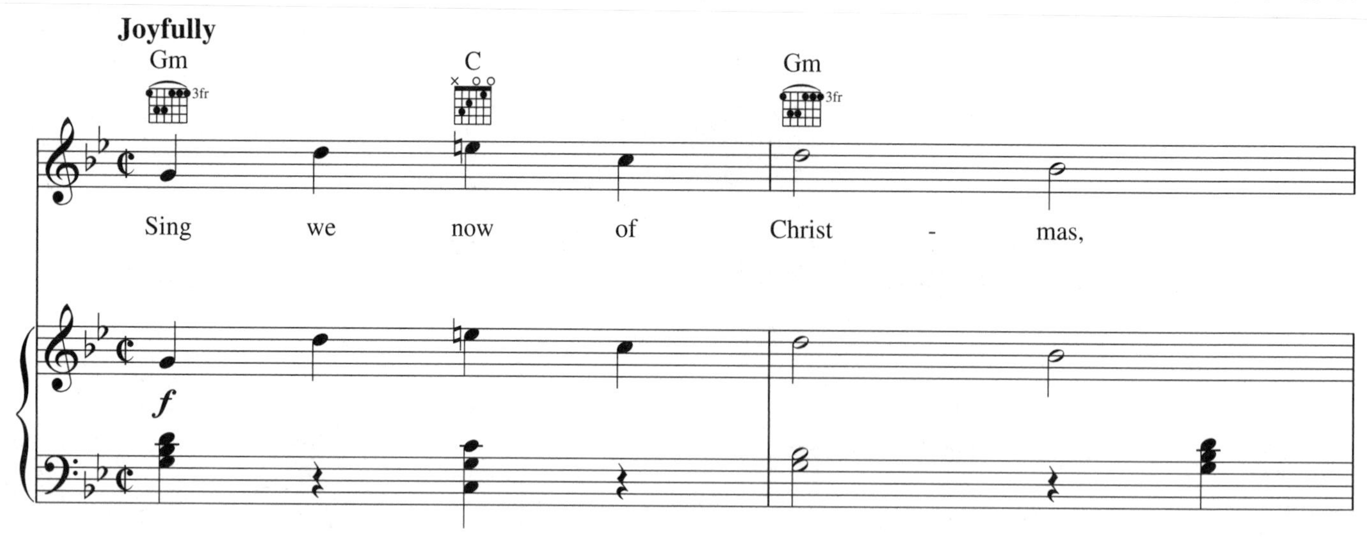


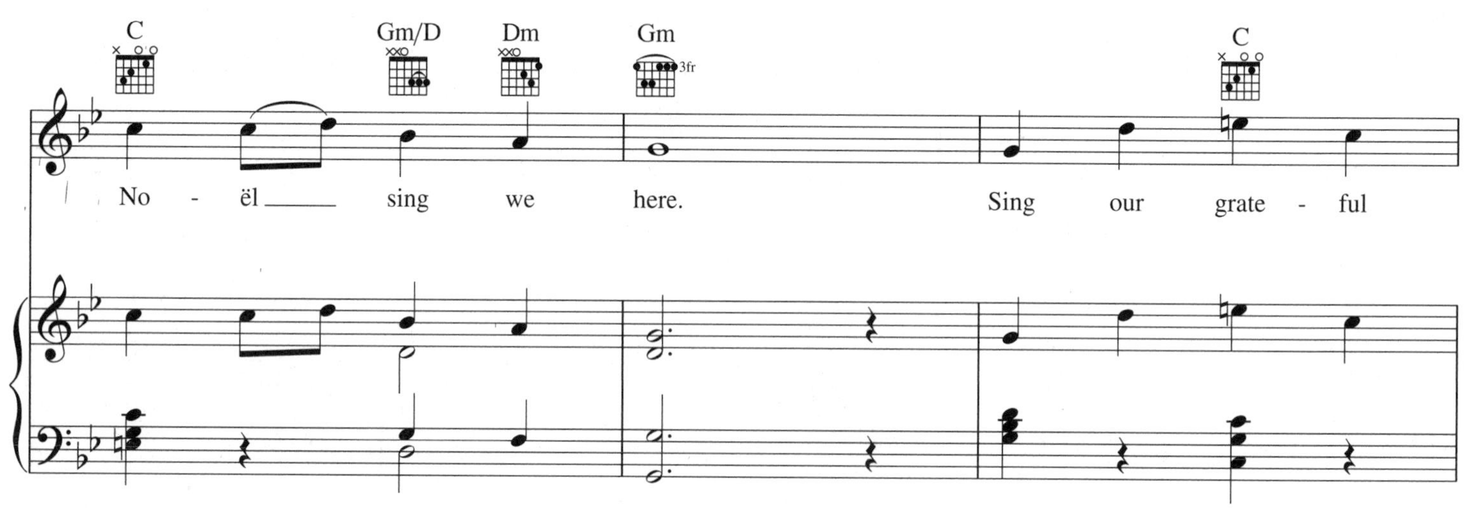


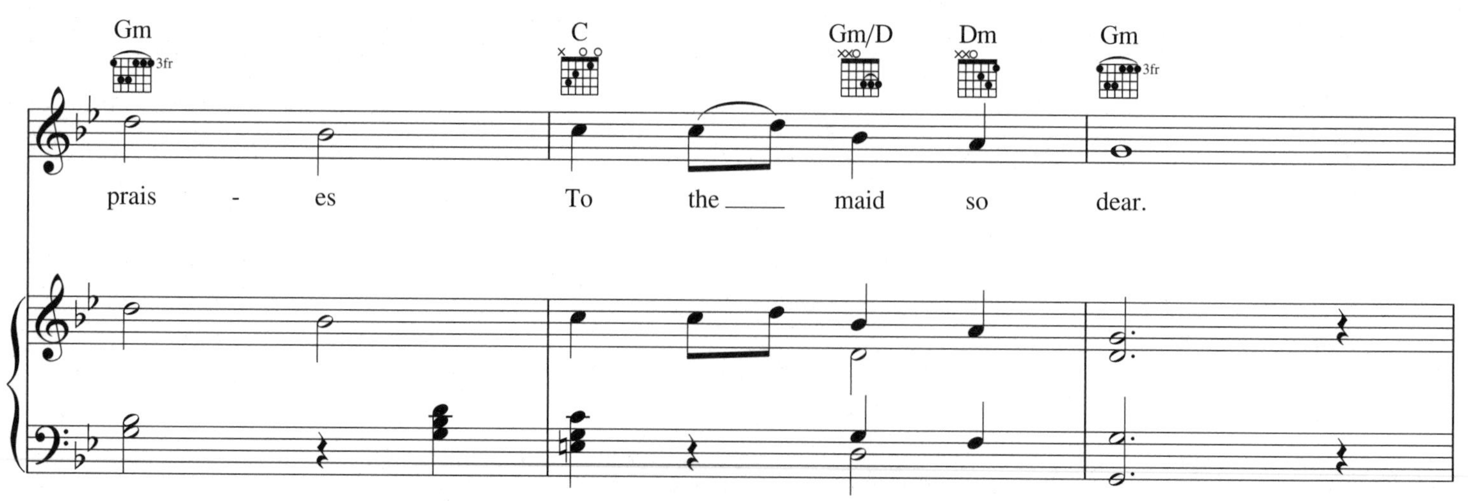

Dm
Gm
3fr
Sing we No - ël! The King is born. No -
C
ël! Sing we now of Christ - mas,
Gm/D
Sing we here No - ël. Sing we now of
Christ - mas, No - ël sing we here.

Gm
C
Gm
C
Gm/D
Dm
3fr
Sing our grate - ful prais - es To the maid so
dear. Sing we No - ël! The
Dm
King is born. No - ël! Sing we now of
Christ - mas, Sing we here No - ël.

# STAR OF THE EAST

Words by GEORGE COOPER
Music by AMANDA KENNEDY

To Coda
C7
F
C7
F
hope of each mor - tal in death's lone - ly night.
bright o'er the cra - dle and bright o'er the
B♭
F/C
D7
Fear - less and tran - quil we look up to thee,
Gm
C7
F
F7
Know - ing thou beam'st thro' e - ter - ni - ty.
B♭
F/C
D7
Help us to fol - low where thou still dost guide

Gm
C7
F
D.S. al Coda
Pil - grims of earth so wide.
CODA
F
F
F♯dim7
Gm
G♯dim7
grave. O star that leads to
o'er us still till
F/A
Bdim7
F/C
D7♭9
Gm7
C7
Am7
D7♭9
God a - bove, Whose rays are peace, are
life hath ceased. Beam on, bright star, sweet
1
Gm7
C7
2
Gm7
C7
F
joy and love, Watch Beth - le - hem star.

# SLEEP, O SLEEP, MY LOVELY CHILD

Traditional Italian Carol

F
Dm7
G7
C13
2fr
F
Gm/F
G/F
F
vine, King di - vine. Close your eyes and
sleep, sweet - ly sleep. Close your eyes, my
Gdim/F
D7
G7
C7
F
Brightly
F
sweet - ly slum - ber.
Son, my dear one.
Fa la la la,
C7
F/C
F
C7
F
Fa la la la la, Fa la la la, Fa la la la.
D.S.
(Last time Fine)
F
Gm/B♭
C7
F
Dm7
Gm
3fr
C7
F
Fa la la la la la, Fa la la la la la, Fa la la la la la, Fa la la la.
Fa la, Fa la, Fa la, Fa la la la.

# THE SNOW LAY ON THE GROUND

Traditional Irish Carol

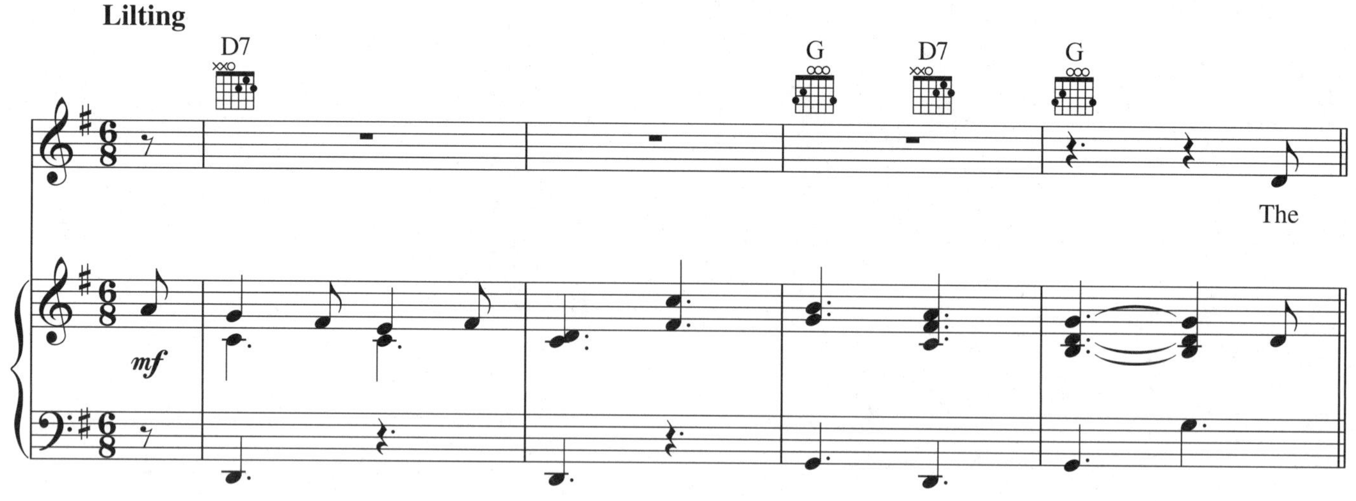


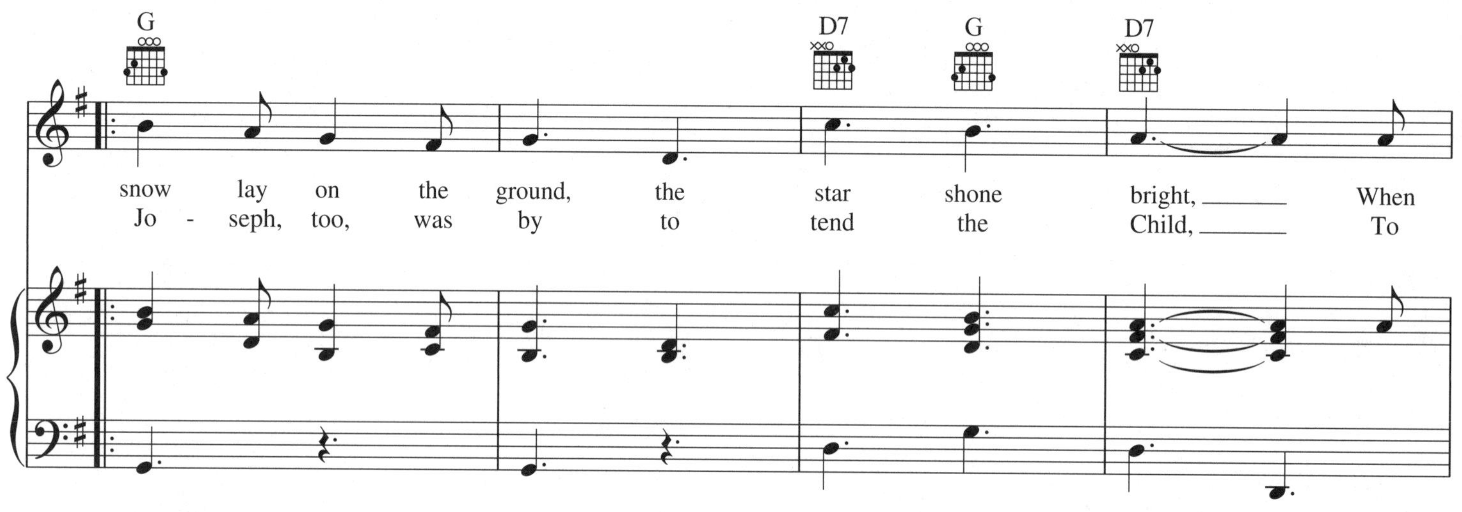


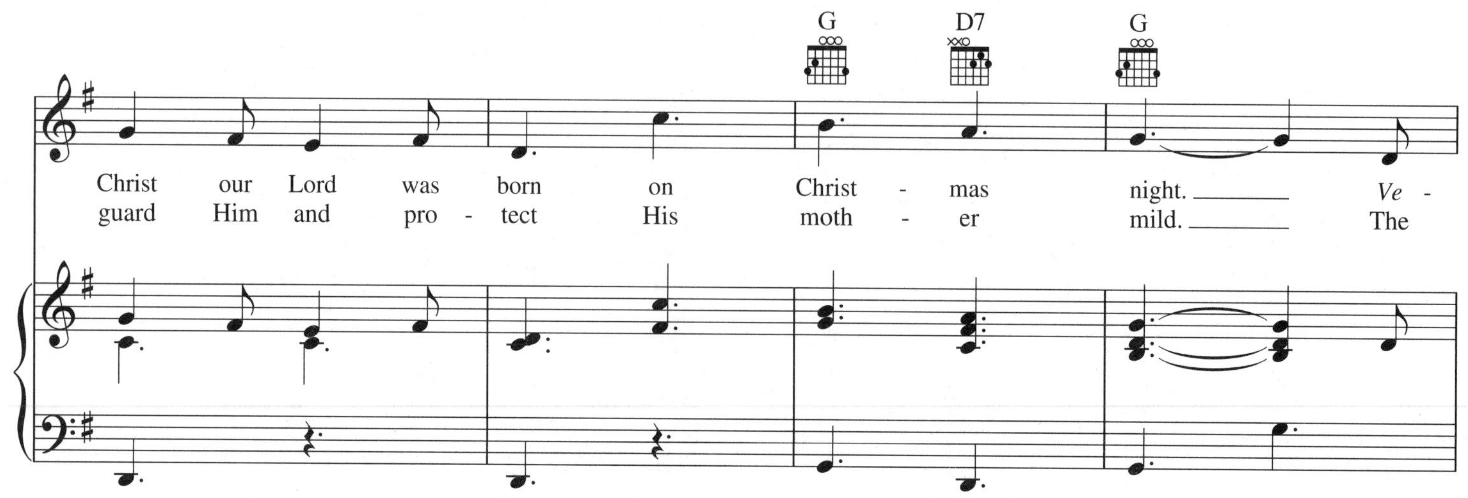

D7
G
D7
ni - te a - do - re - mus Do - mi - num;
an - gels hov - ered 'round and sang this song:
Ve -
G
D7
G
ni - te a - do - re - mus Do - mi - num.
Ve -
Am
E7
Am
ni - te a - do - re - mus Do - mi - num,
Ve -
D7
G
D7
1
G
2
G
ni - te a - do - re - mus Do - mi - num.
Saint
num.

# THE SON OF MARY

Traditional Catalonian Carol

Moderately

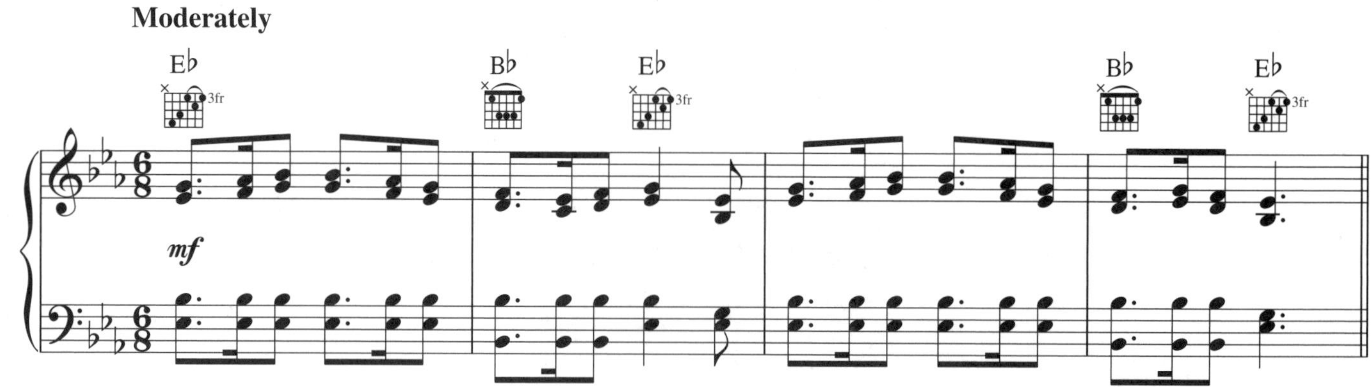


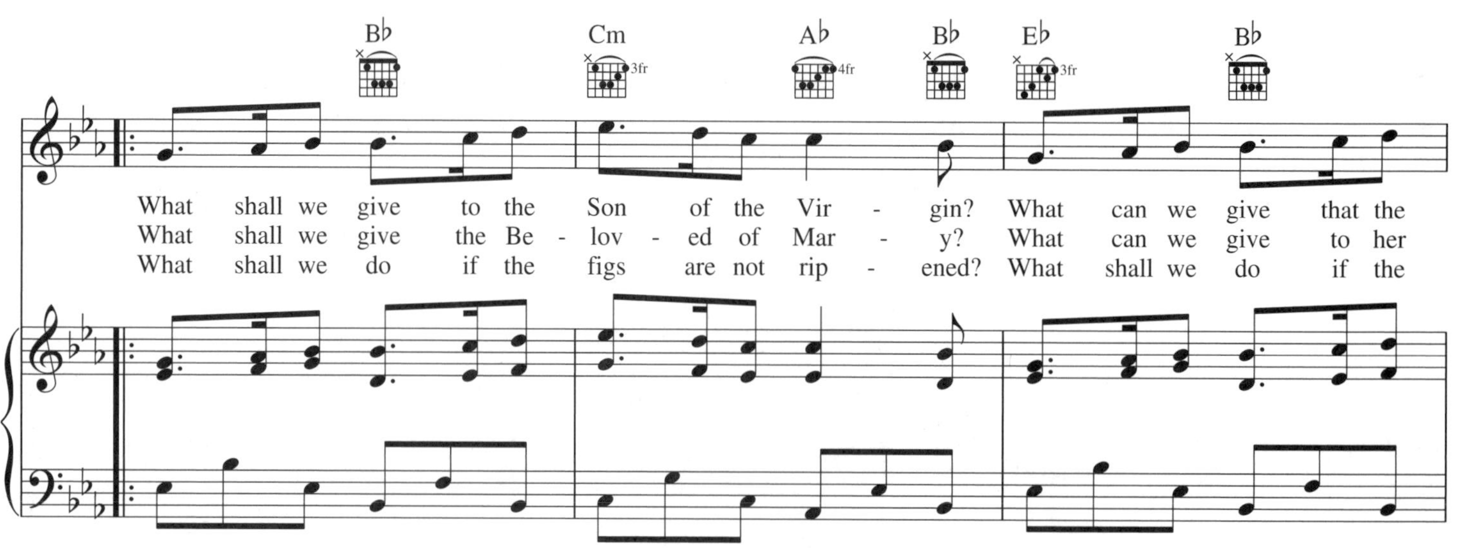

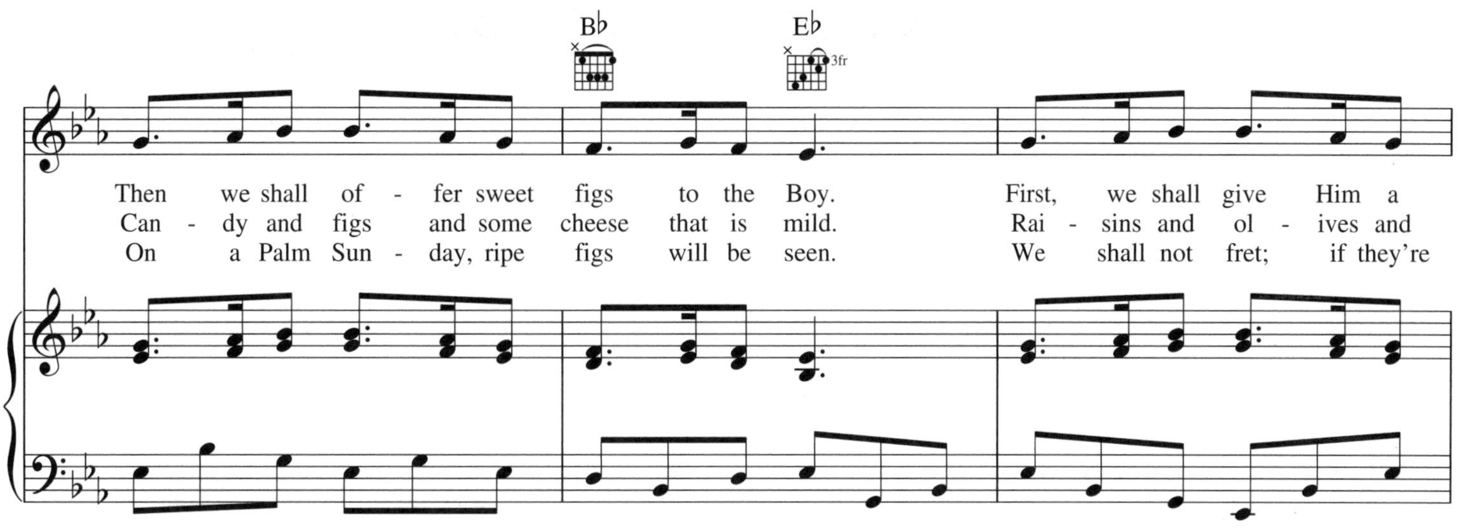
B♭
E♭
3fr
Then we shall of - fer sweet figs to the Boy. First, we shall give Him a
Can - dy and figs and some cheese that is mild. Rai - sins and ol - ives and
On a Palm Sun - day, ripe figs will be seen. We shall not fret; if they're

B♭
E♭
3fr
1, 2
tray full of rai - sins, then we shall of - fer sweet figs to the Boy.
nut - meats and hon - ey, Can - dy and figs and some cheese that is mild.
not ripe for Eas - ter, On a Palm Sun - day, ripe

3
B♭
E♭
3fr
figs will be seen.
rall.

# STILL, STILL, STILL

Salzburg Melody, c.1819
Traditional Austrian Text

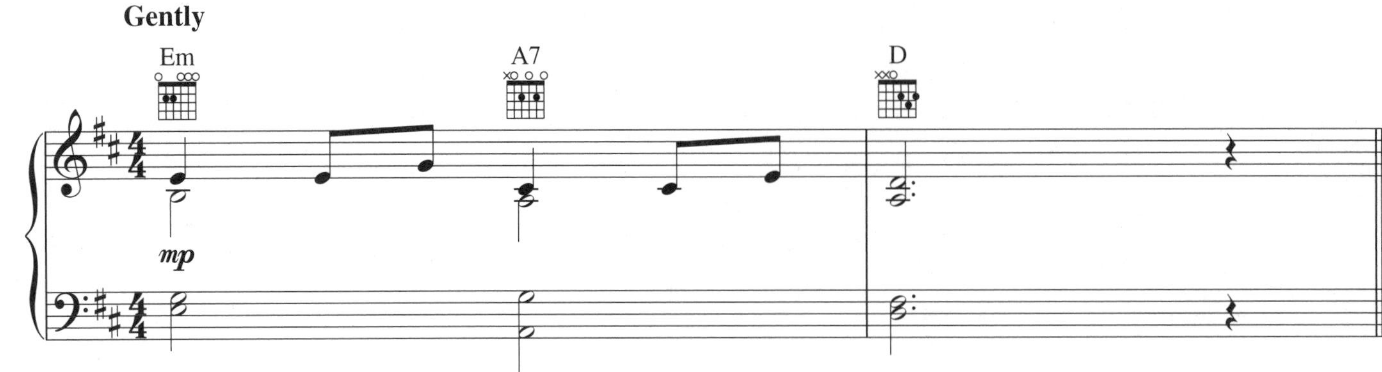


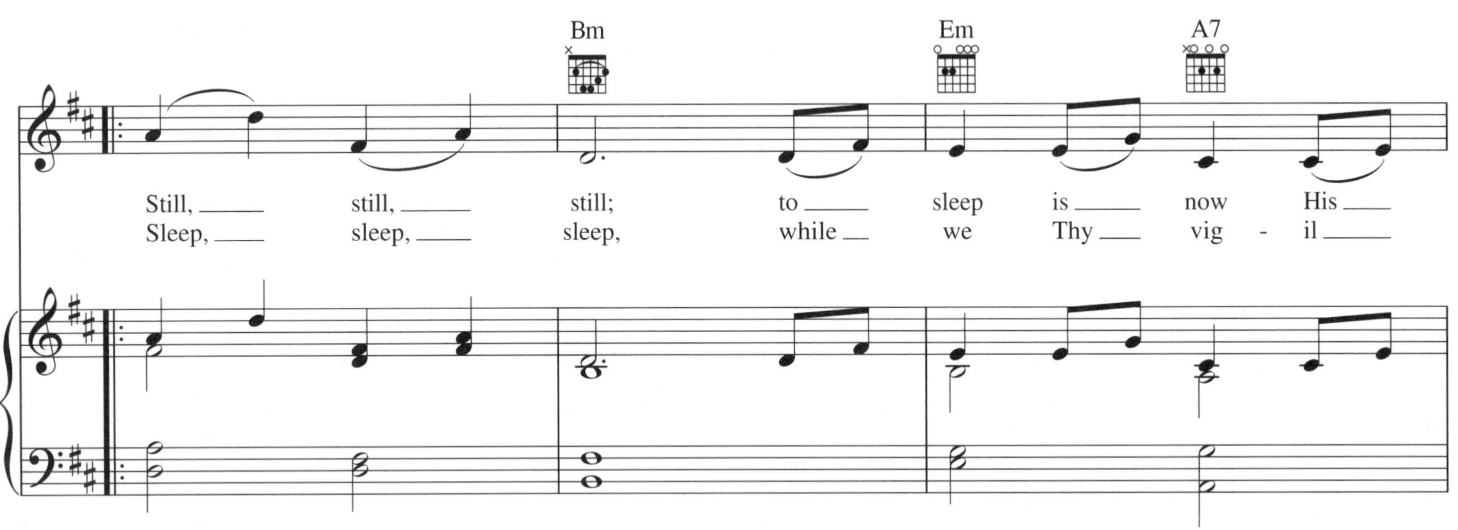


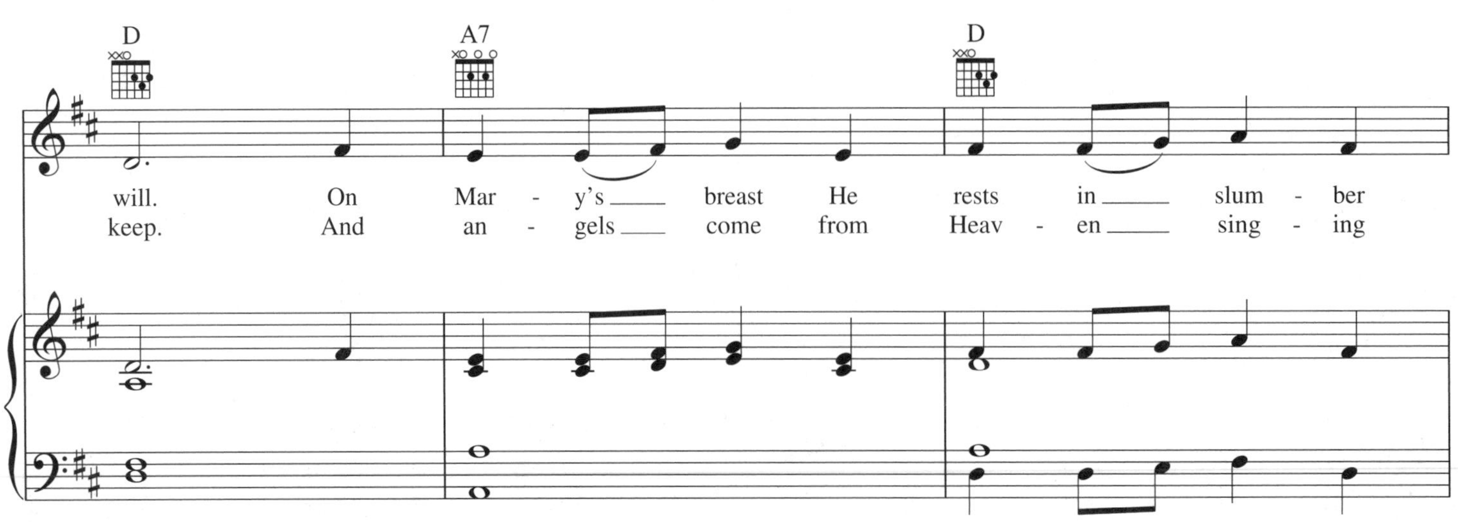

A7
D
while we pray in end - less num - ber.
songs of ju - bi - la - tion bring - ing
D/C♯
Bm
Bm/A
Em/G
A7
Still, still, still; to sleep is now His
sleep, sleep, sleep, while we Thy vig - il
1
2
D
D
D/C♯
will.
keep.
Sleep, sleep,
Bm
Bm/A
Em/G
A7
D
sleep, while we Thy vig - il keep.
rall.

# SUSANI

14th Century German Carol

Dm
C
F
su - sa - ni!
And let the joy - ful
With harp and chimes your
With strings and or - gan
And praise to God, our
C
F
Dm
trum - pets ring!
Sav - ior greet!
raise the cry!
heav'n - ly guide!
Al - le - lu - ia! Al -
B♭
C
F
C
F
le - lu - ia! Of Mar - y we sing, and
Dm
C
1 - 3
F
4
F
Christ, her Son.
Come
O
Sing
Son.

# SUSSEX CAROL

Traditional English Carol

G
C
G
D
G
D
D/C
hear the news the an - gels bring. News of great
our Re - deem - er made us glad. When from our
life and health come in its place. An - gels and
made the an - gels sing this night. "Glo - ry to
D/B
7fr
C
D
G
C
G
joy, news of great mirth, news of our
sin He set us free, all for to
men with joy may sing, all for to
God and peace to men, now and for -
C
D
G
C
mer - ci - ful King's birth.
gain our li - ber - ty.
see the new - born King.
ev - er - more. A - men."
G
D
1 - 3
G
4
G
Then
When
All

# THERE'S A SONG IN THE AIR

Words and Music by JOSIAH G. HOLLAND
and KARL P. HARRINGTON

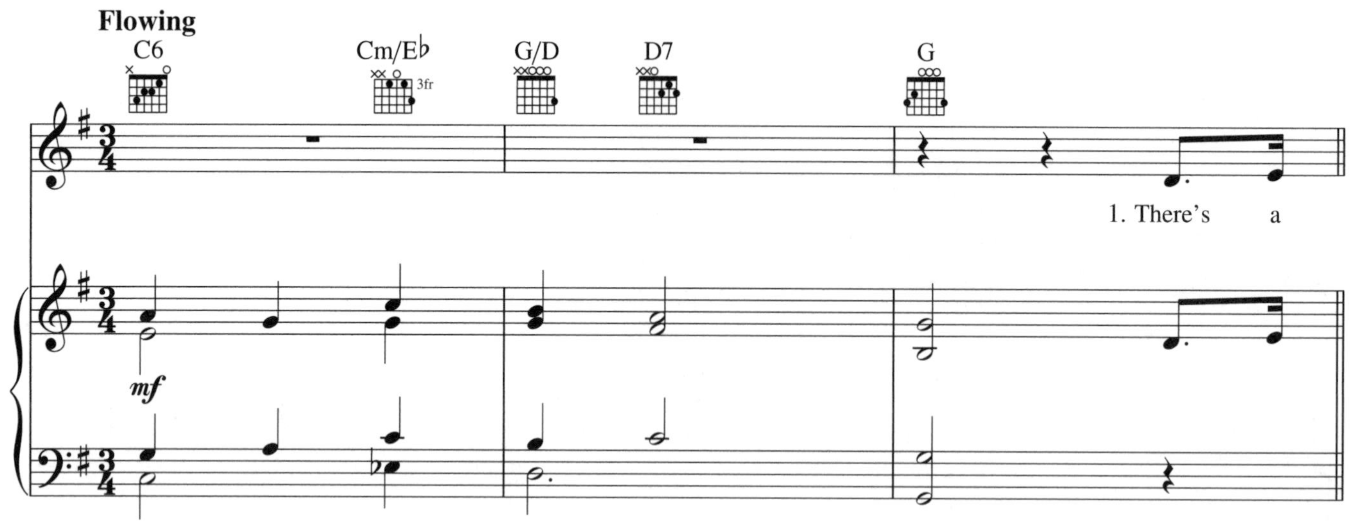

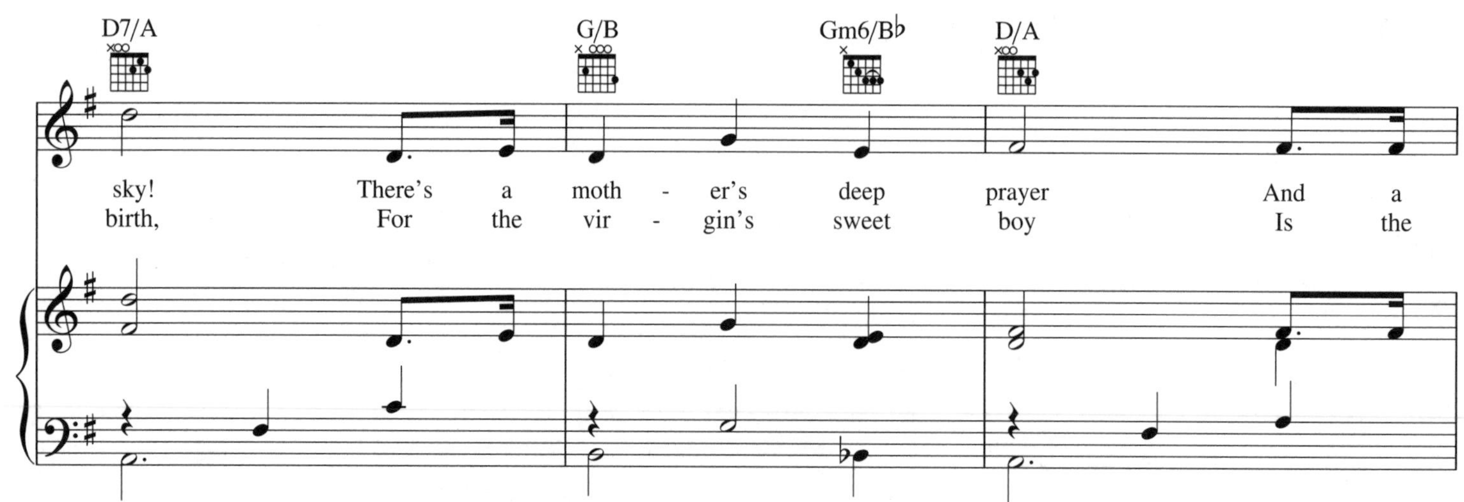

*Additional Lyrics*

3. In the light of that star
Lie the ages impearled,
And that song from afar
Has swept over the world.
Ev'ry hearth is aflame, and the angels sing
In the homes of the nations that Jesus is King!

4. We rejoice in the light,
And we echo the song
That comes down thro' the night
From the heavenly throng.
Ay! we shout to the lovely evangel they bring
And we greet in His cradle our Savior and King!

# TO US IS BORN A LITTLE CHILD

Traditional German Carol

G D F♯
mer - ry sea - son is, Babe
world, this Babe, I say, doth
hem the shep - herds fare, and
D A G A D
Je - sus our de - light and bliss.
put thee to the blush to - day.
first - lings of their flock they bear.
O
G D G
Je - sus, dar - ling of my heart, how
D A F♯m G A
1, 2 D
3 D
rich in mer - cy, Babe, Thou art. art.

# TOURO-LOURO-LOURO

Traditional French Lyrics
Music by NICOLAS SABOLY

G D G D
night. "Will you go there?" "No, I can - not!" "Go with me
old. "Please let me rest." "No rest for you." "I must find
smiles! "Good day to you!" (He's laugh - ing now!) "Good day to
G D G D G D
there?" "No, I can - not." O Wil - liam, O Wil -
rest." "No rest for you." O farm - er, O farm -
you!" (Jo - seph's so proud!) O Mar - y, O Mar -
G C D7 G
liam, if I nev - er should re - turn, say a psalm to
er, give me shel - ter for the night, in the hay - loft
y, may your name be ev - er blessed, for the Child that
C D7 G Em
give me bless - ing! Still, I must
I'd be sleep - ing. Shel - ter, I do
Heav - en sent thee! Saint Jo - seph,

G D G

go, Yea, ___ I must go; though the ___
pray, just ___ for this day; for I'm ___
too, bless - ings un - to you! For the ___

D7 G D7 G D7

jour - ney will ___ be long, still I must go, yea, I ___ must
near to freez - ing now. Don't let me die! Don't let ___ me
love - ly Child ___ so dear, that we all love, that we ___ all

G Em C G

go.
die!
love.

C G | 1, 2 D G | 3 D G

Tou - ro - lou - ro -

# 'TWAS THE NIGHT BEFORE CHRISTMAS

Words by CLEMENT CLARK MOORE
Music by F. HENRI KLICKMAN

Cmaj7
Dm7
Em7
Cm6/E♭
G/D
stock - ings were hung by the chim - ney with care, In
way to the win - dow I flew like a flash, Tore
Am
Am7
D9
G13
G7
D9/A
G7
4fr
3fr
4fr
hopes that Saint Nich - o - las soon would be there. The
o - pen the shut - ters and threw up the sash. The
C
Gm/B♭
A7
Dm7
G7
chil - dren were nes - tled all snug in their beds, While
moon, on the breast of the new - fall - en snow, Gave a
F♯m7♭5
B7
Gm7
C7
4fr
vi - sions of sug - ar plums danced thro' their heads. And
lus - tre of mid - day to ob - jects be - low. When

*Additional Lyrics*

3. With a little old driver so lively and quick,
I knew in a moment it must be St. Nick.
More rapid than eagles his coursers they came,
And he whistled, and shouted, and called them by name:
"Now, Dasher! Now, Dancer! Now, Prancer! Now, Vixen!
On, Comet! On, Cupid! On, Donder and Blitzen!
To the top of the porch, to the top of the wall!
Now dash away, dash away, dash away all!"

4. As dry leaves that before the wild hurricane fly,
When they meet with an obstacle, mount to the sky,
So up to the house-top the coursers they flew,
With the sleigh full of toys, and St. Nicholas, too.
And then in a twinkling I heard on the roof
The prancing and pawing of each little hoof.
As I drew in my head, and was turning around,
Down the chimney St. Nicholas came with a bound.

5. He was dressed all in fur from his head to his foot,
And his clothes were all tarnished with ashes and soot;
A bundle of toys he had flung on his back,
And he looked like a peddler just opening his pack.
His eyes how they twinkled! His dimples how merry!
His cheeks were like roses, his nose like a cherry.
His droll little mouth was drawn up like a bow,
And the beard of his chin was as white as the snow.

6. The stump of a pipe he held tight in his teeth,
And the smoke, it encircled his head like a wreath.
He had a broad face, and a round little belly
That shook, when he laughed, like a bowl full of jelly.
He was chubby and plump, a right jolly old elf,
And I laughed when I saw him, in spite of myself.
A wink of his eye, and a twist of his head,
Soon gave me to know I had nothing to dread.

7. He spoke not a word, but went straight to his work,
And filled all the stockings; then turned with a jerk,
And laying his finger aside of his nose,
And giving a nod, up the chimney he rose.
He sprang to his sleigh, to his team gave a whistle,
And away they all fled like the down of a thistle;
But I heard him exclaim, ere he drove out of sight:
"Happy Christmas to all, and to all a Good-night!"

# THE TWELVE DAYS OF CHRISTMAS

Traditional English Carol

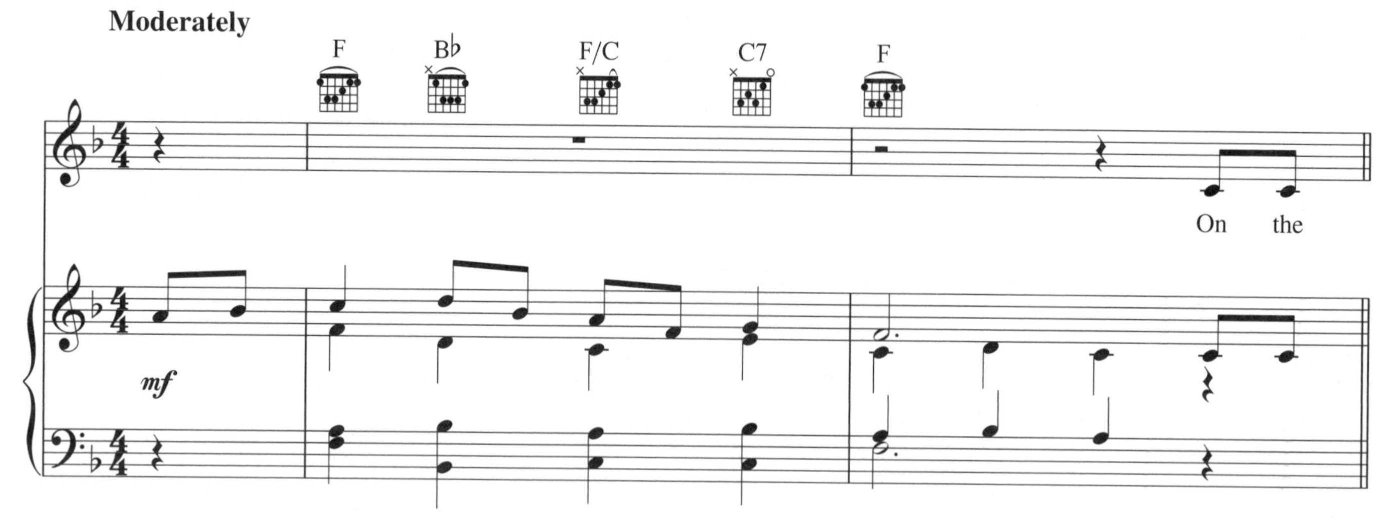

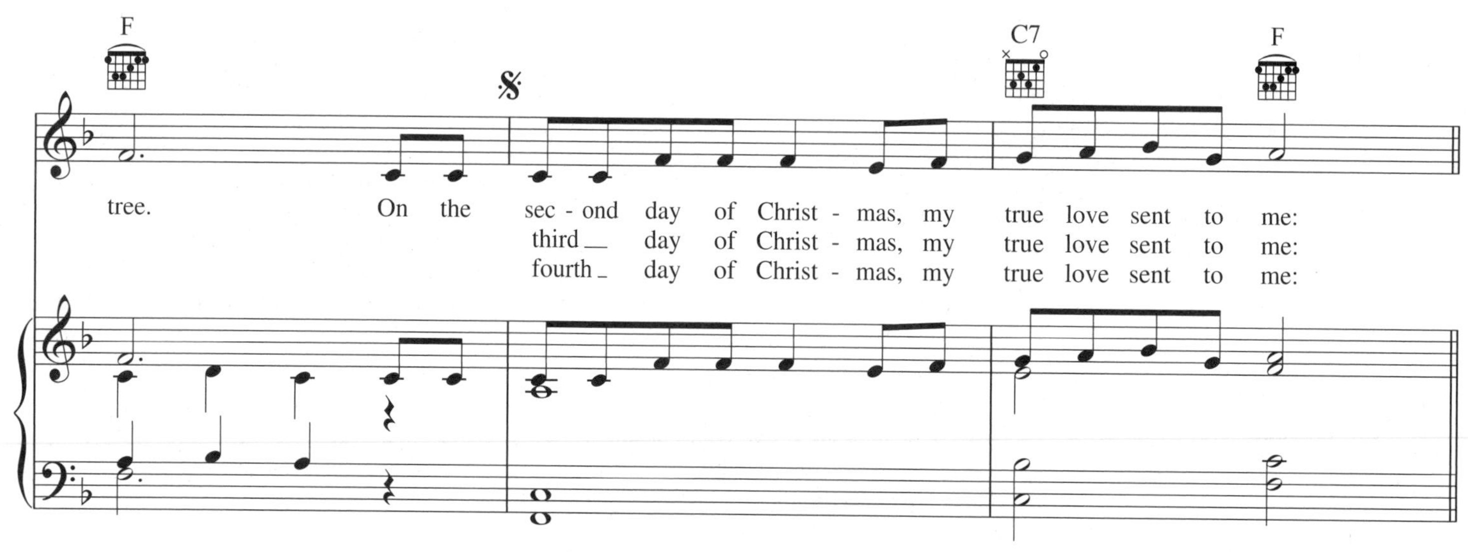

C7
F
B♭
F/C
C7
Repeat as needed
Two tur - tle - doves
Three French hens,
Four call - ing birds,
and a par - tridge in a pear
1, 2
3
F
D.S.
tree.
On the
On the
tree.
On the fifth day of Christ - mas, my
C7
F
G7
C
true love sent to me: Five gold rings!
F
Gm
3fr
C7
Four call - ing birds, three French hens, two tur - tle - doves, and a

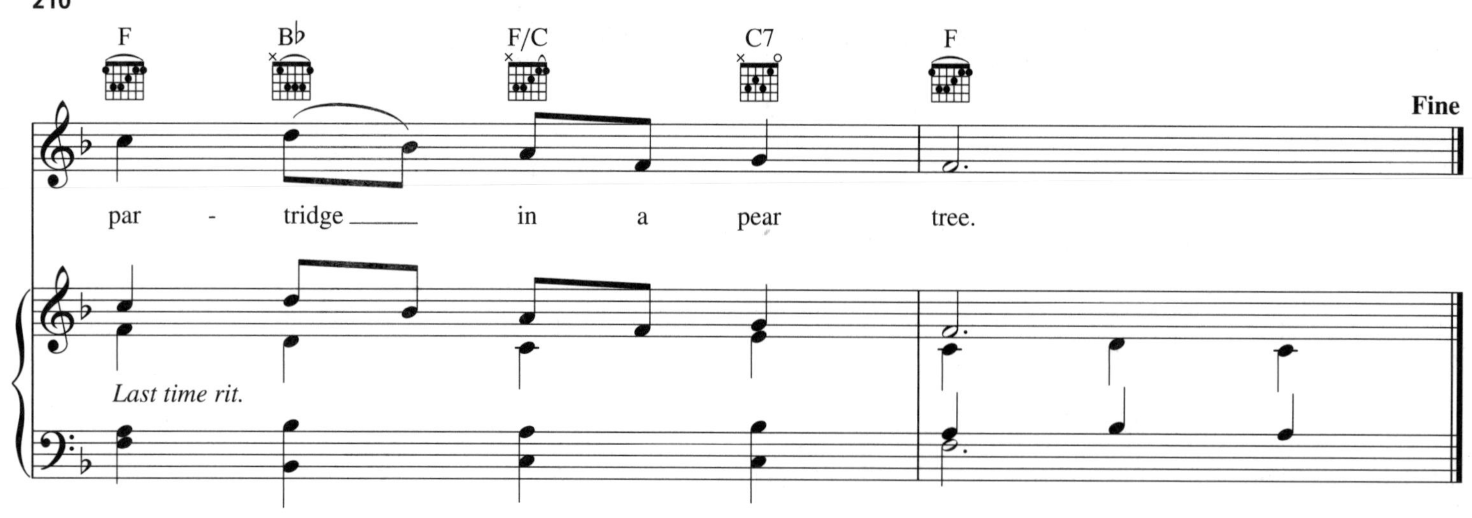
F
B♭
F/C
C7
F
Fine
par - tridge in a pear tree.
Last time rit.

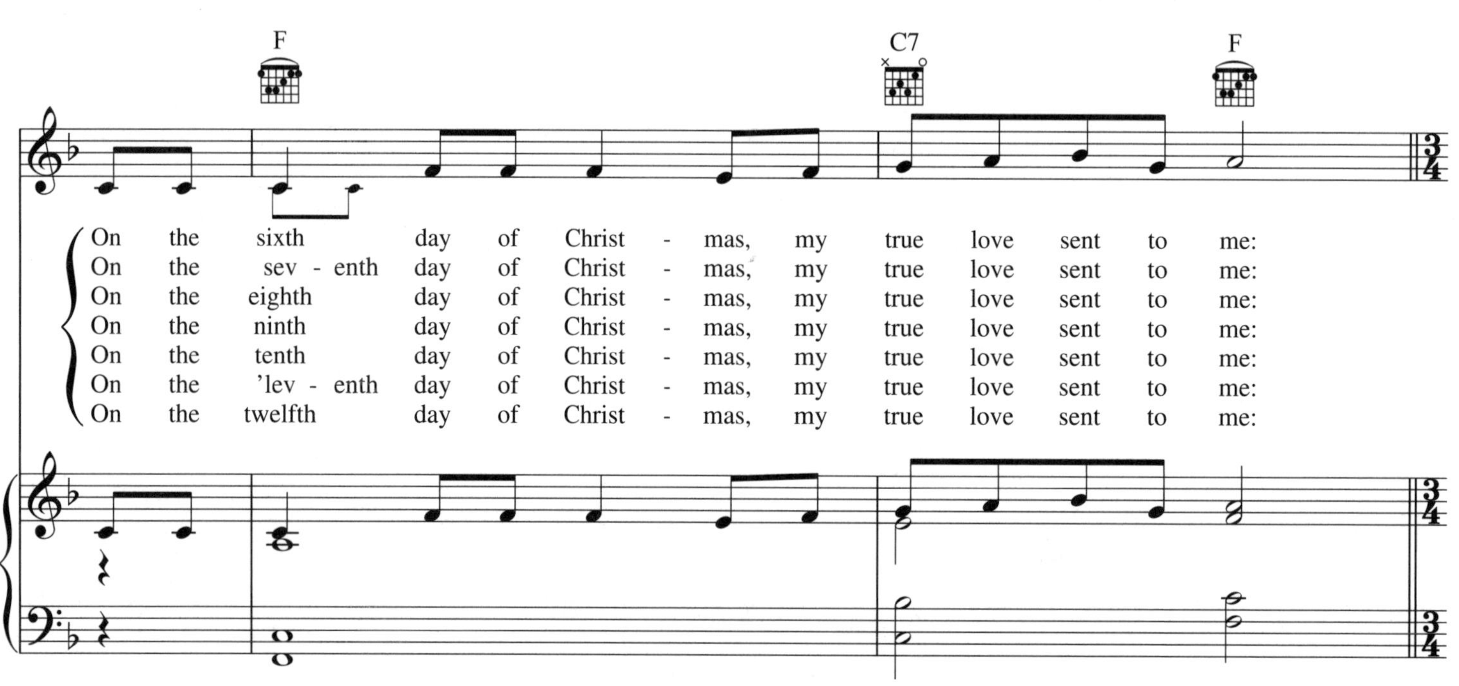
F
C7
F
On the sixth day of Christ - mas, my true love sent to me:
On the sev - enth day of Christ - mas, my true love sent to me:
On the eighth day of Christ - mas, my true love sent to me:
On the ninth day of Christ - mas, my true love sent to me:
On the tenth day of Christ - mas, my true love sent to me:
On the 'lev - enth day of Christ - mas, my true love sent to me:
On the twelfth day of Christ - mas, my true love sent to me:

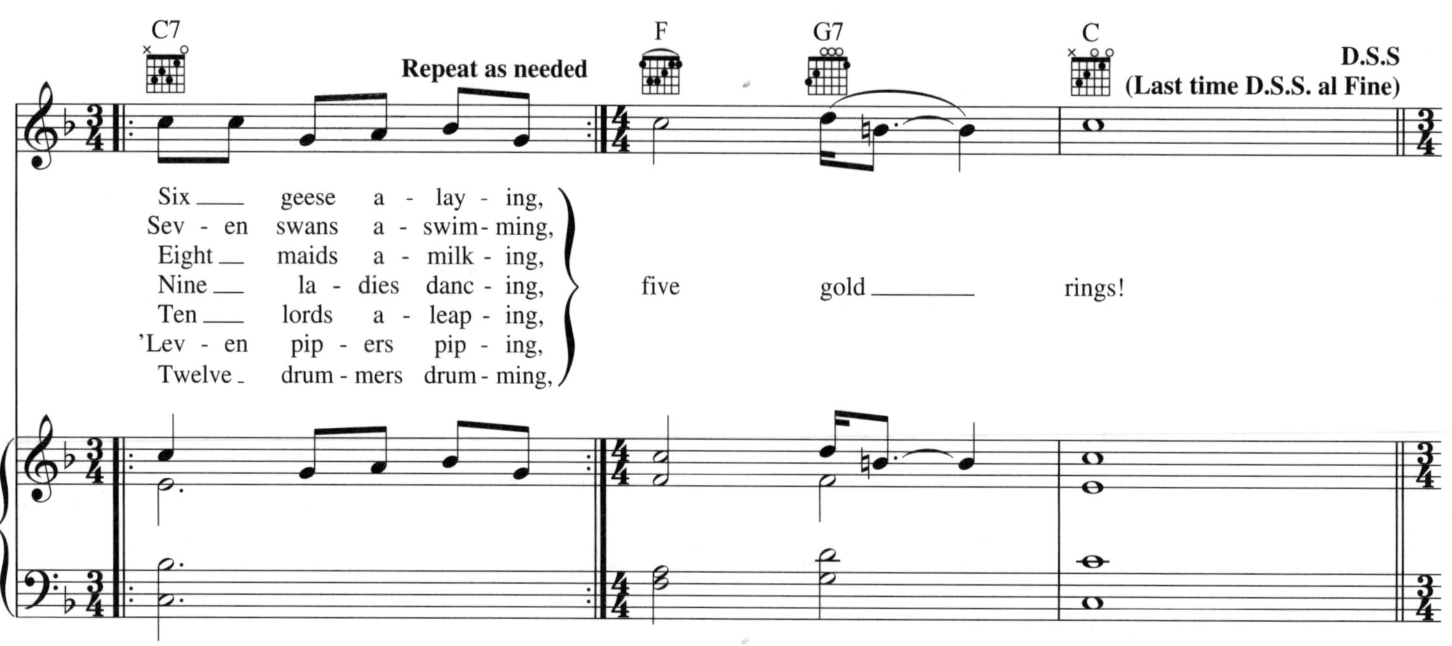
C7
Repeat as needed
F
G7
C
D.S.S
(Last time D.S.S. al Fine)
Six geese a - lay - ing,
Sev - en swans a - swim - ming,
Eight maids a - milk - ing,
Nine la - dies danc - ing,
Ten lords a - leap - ing,
'Lev - en pip - ers pip - ing,
Twelve drum - mers drum - ming,
five gold rings!

# WASSAIL, WASSAIL

Old English Air

**Moderately**

F Dm C B♭ C F

*mf*

C F Dm C B♭ C F

Was - sail, Was - sail all ___ o - ver the town! Our
was - s'ling bowl with a toast ___ with - in, come,
but - ler bring us a bowl ___ of your best, and

C F Dm C F Am

bread it is white and our ale it is brown. Our bowl is made of the
fill it up now un - to ___ the brim. Come, fill it up that we
we hope your soul in ___ heav - en shall rest. But if you bring us a

Gm Dm A Gm Dm | 1, 2 Gm C F | 3 Gm C F

ma - ple tree, so here my good fel - low, I'll drink to thee. The
may ___ all see, with the was - sail - ing bowl, I'll drink to thee. Come
bowl ___ too small, then down shall go but - ler and bowl and all.

# UP ON THE HOUSETOP

Words and Music by
B.R. HANBY

A♭ E♭/G B♭7 E♭
All for the lit - tle ones, Christ - mas joys.
One that will o - pen and shut her eyes.
A♭ E♭ B♭7
Ho, ho, ho! Who would - n't go! Ho, ho, ho!
E♭ E♭/D♭ A♭/C E♭/B♭ A♭
Who would - n't go! Up on the house - top, click, click, click,
E♭ E♭/G B♭7 E♭
Down through the chim - ney with good Saint Nick.

# A VIRGIN UNSPOTTED

Traditional English Carol

*Additional Lyrics*

3. Then presently after, the shepherds did spy
   Vast numbers of angels to stand in the sky;
   They joyfully talked and sweetly did sing:
   "To God be all glory, our heavenly King."
   *Refrain*

4. To teach us humility all this was done,
   And learn we from thence haughty pride for to shun;
   A manger His cradle who came from above,
   The great God of mercy, of peace and of love.
   *Refrain*

# WASSAIL SONG

Traditional English Carol

B♭
E♭/B♭
Cm
A♭
wan - d'ring, so fair to be seen.
chil - dren, whom you have seen be - fore.
chil - dren, who wan - der in the mire.
chil - dren, that round the ta - ble go.
Love and joy come to
E♭
E♭/D
E♭/C
Cm/B♭
E♭
Cm
you, and to you glad Christ - mas, too; and God bless you and
A♭
B♭
E♭
B♭7
E♭
C
send you a hap - py New Year, and God send you a
F
B♭7
1 - 3
E♭
4
E♭
hap - py New Year.
We
Good
God
Year.

# WATCHMAN, TELL US OF THE NIGHT

Words by JOHN BOWRING
Music by JACOB HINTZE

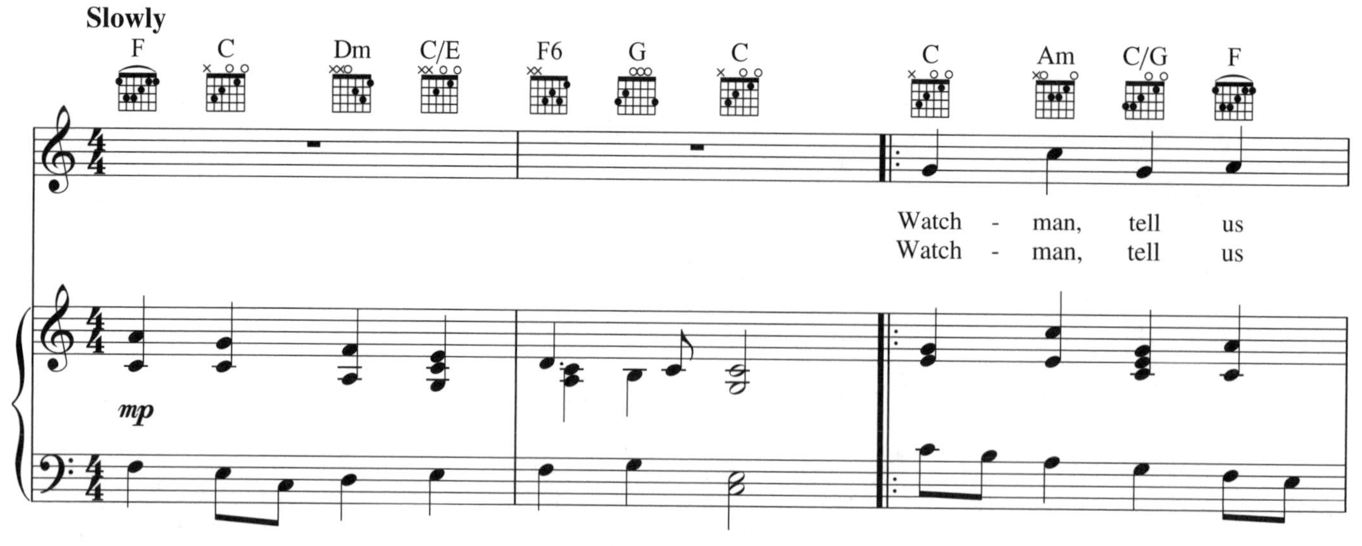


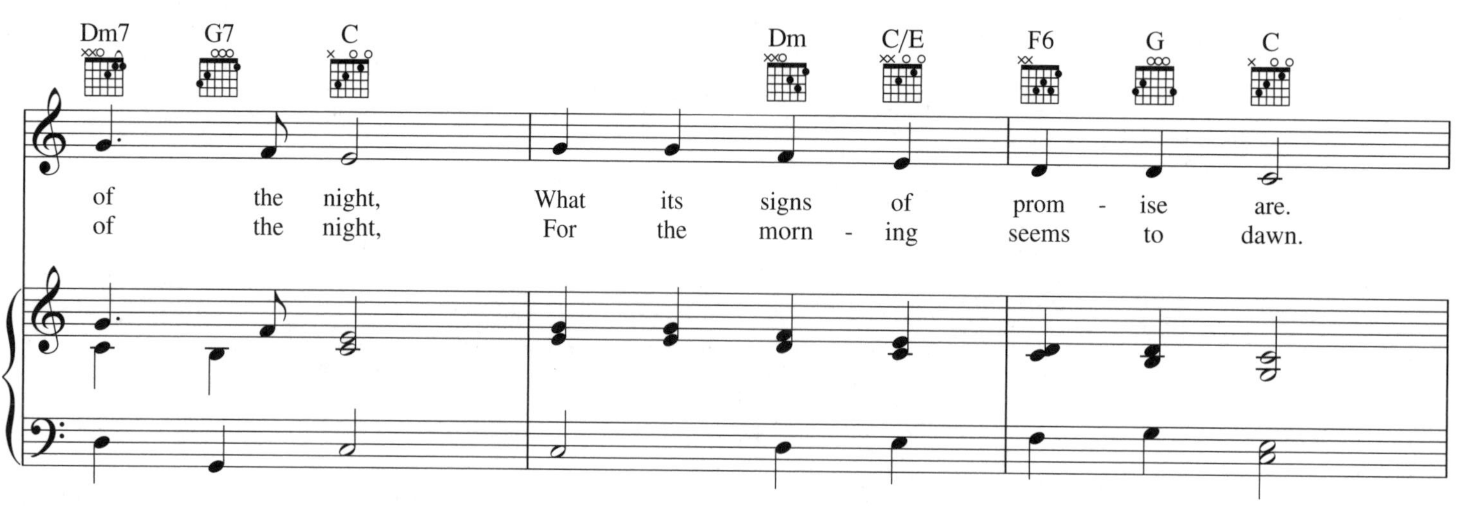


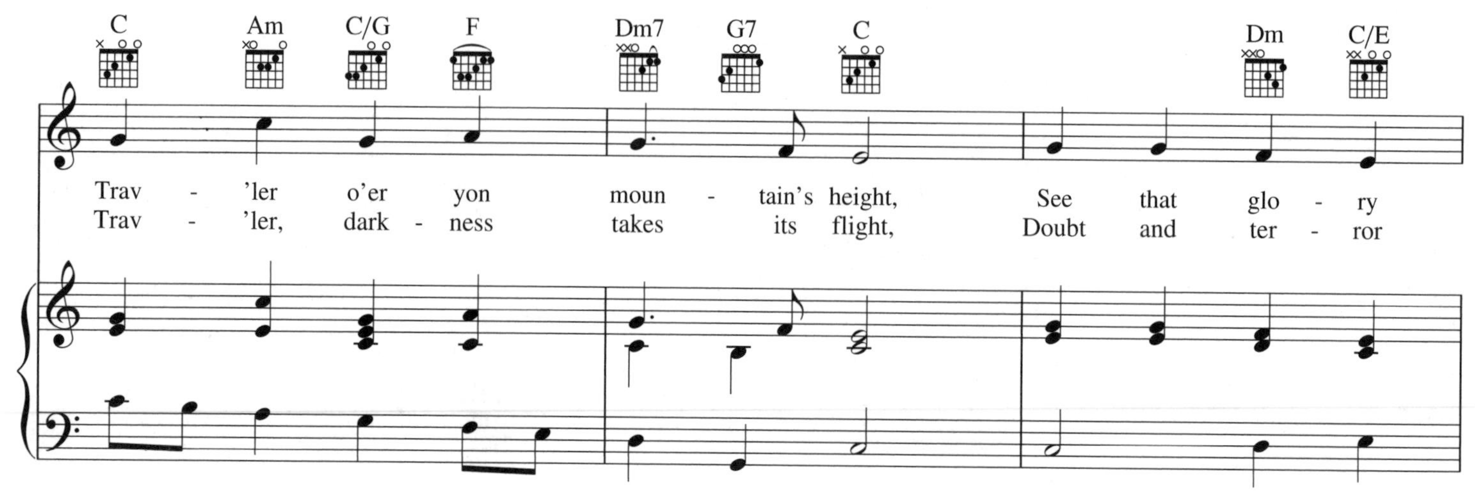

F6
G
C
G
C
Em
Am7
D7/A
G
beam - ing star. Watch - man, does its beau - teous ray
are with - drawn. Watch - man, let thy wan - d'rings cease,

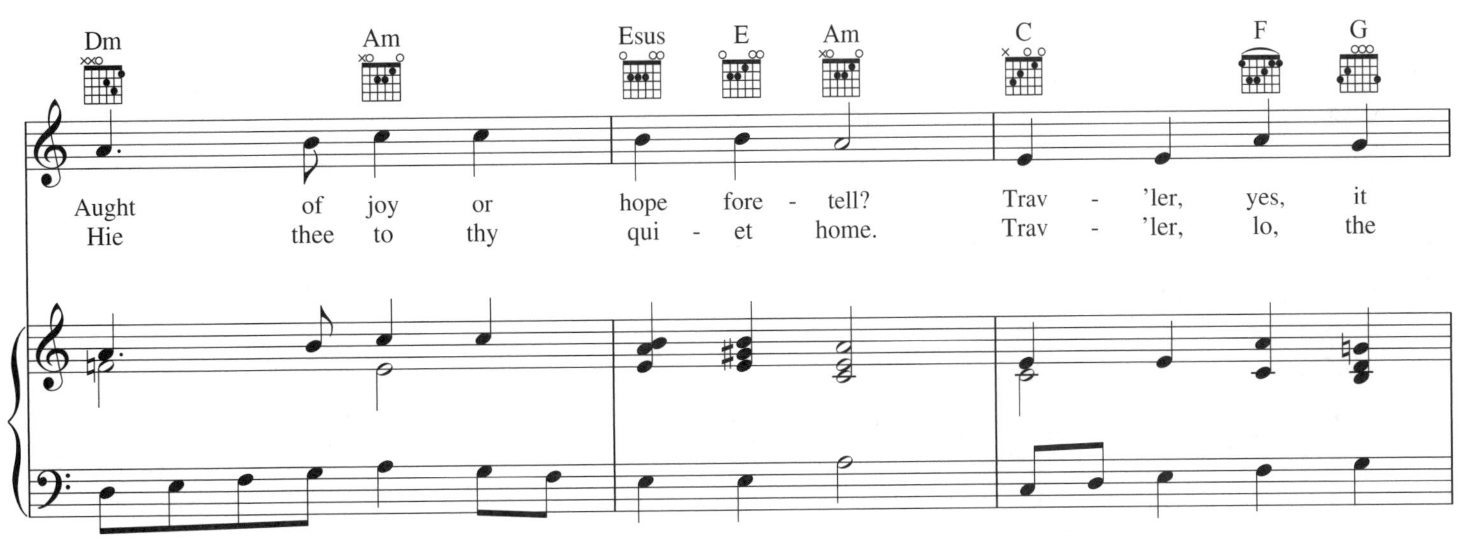
Dm
Am
Esus
E
Am
C
F
G
Aught of joy or hope fore - tell? Trav - 'ler, yes, it
Hie thee to thy qui - et home. Trav - 'ler, lo, the

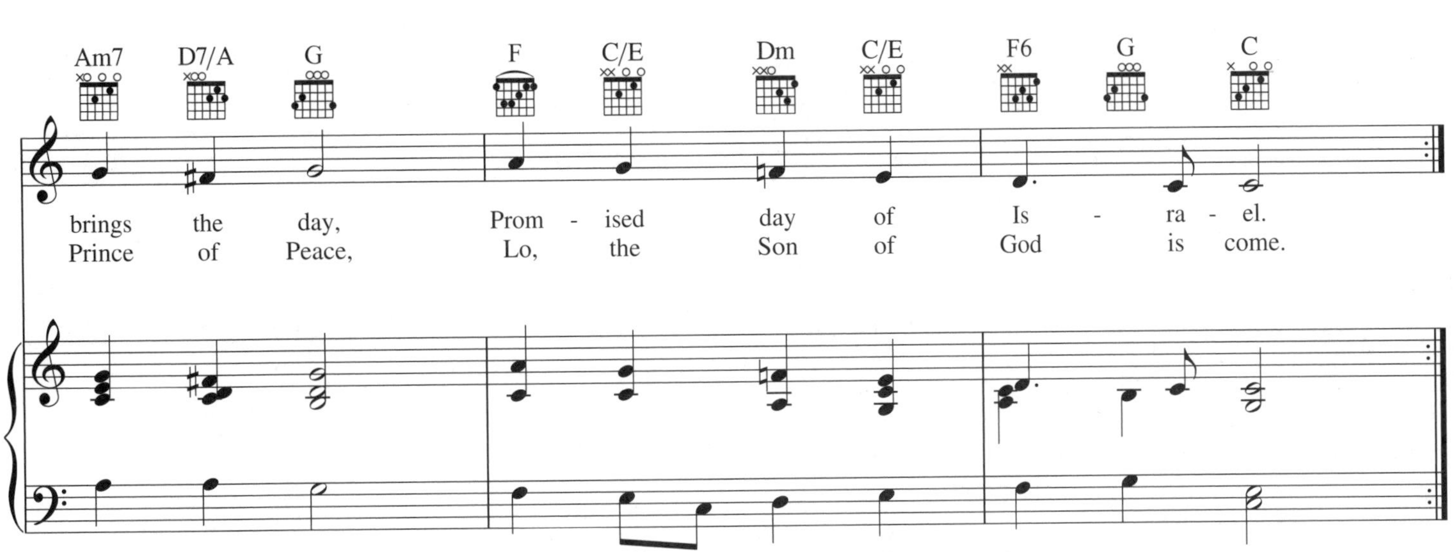
Am7
D7/A
G
F
C/E
Dm
C/E
F6
G
C
brings the day, Prom - ised day of Is - ra - el.
Prince of Peace, Lo, the Son of God is come.

# WE ARE SINGING

Traditional Venezuelan Folk Song

Bm
Em
A
Mer - ry Eve of Christ - mas, to Thee, In - fant
D
G
King. All our ex - pec - ta - tion,
Beam - ing through the dark - ness,
Night of cel - e - bra - tion,
A
D
all our char - i - ty,
flood - ing rays so bright,
night of Je - sus' birth,
all our con - so -
shin - ing on the
night of ho - ly
G
A
D
la - tion, Child dear in Thee.
cra - dle, on the glo - rious night.
splen - dor, and re - deem - ing love.

A
D
A
Sing - ing we are sing - ing, lov - ing praise we
D
G
bring, Mer - ry Eve of Christ - mas,
A
D
Bm
Mer - ry Eve of Christ - mas, Mer - ry Eve of
Em
A
1, 2
D
3
D
Christ - mas, to Thee, In - fant King. King.

# WE WISH YOU A MERRY CHRISTMAS

Traditional English Folk Song

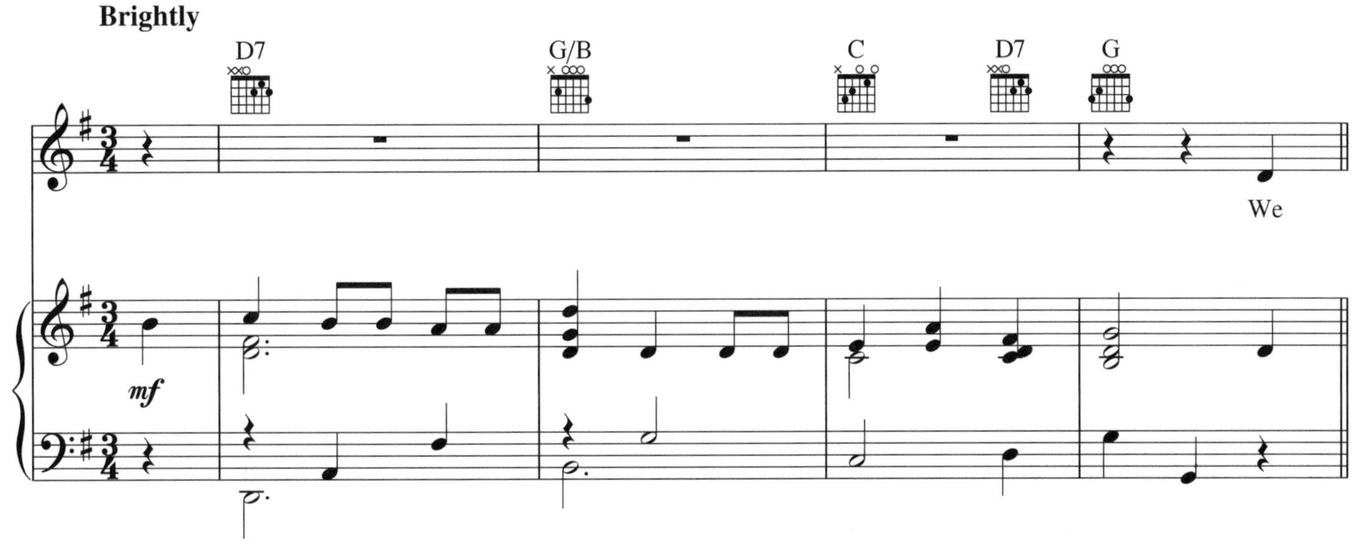


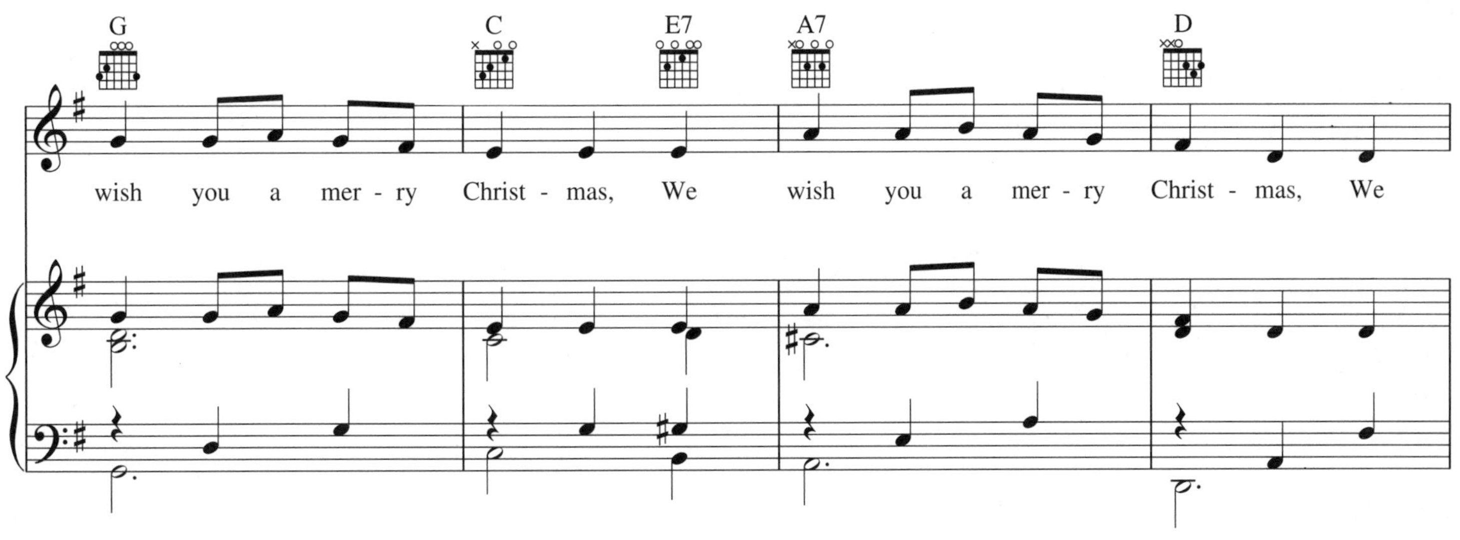


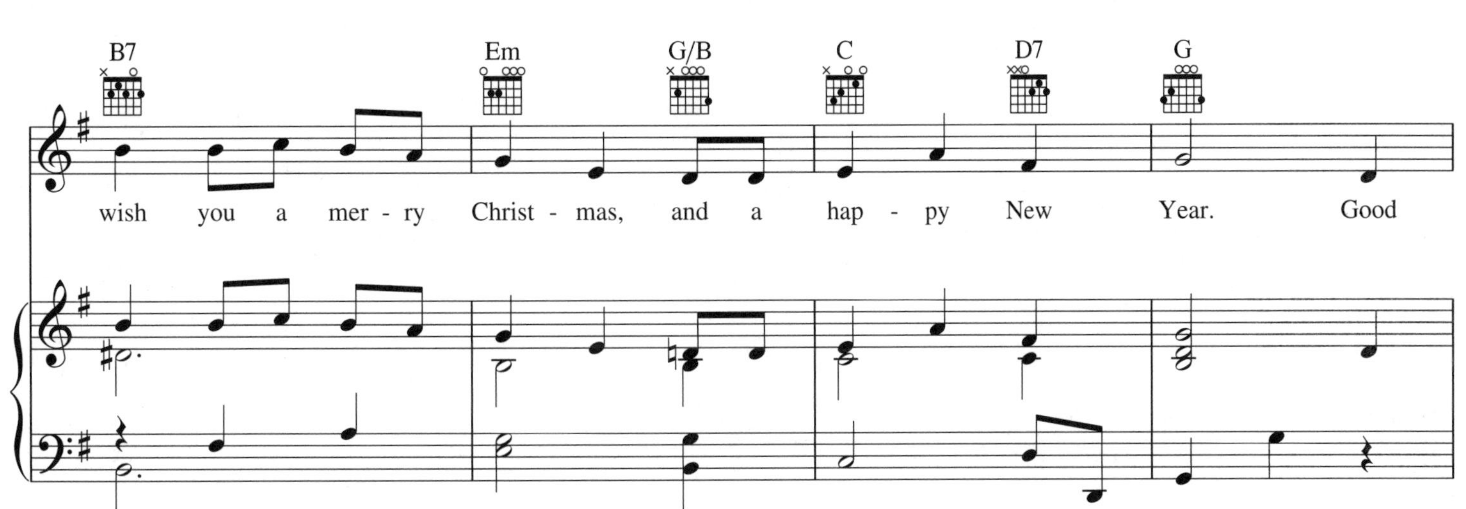

Bm7
A7
D7
G
tid - ings we bring to you and your kin, Good
D7
G
C
D7
G
tid - ings for Christ - mas and a hap - py New Year. We
C
E7
A7
D
all know that San - ta's com - ing, We all know that San - ta's com - ing, We
B7
Em
G/B
C
D7
G
all know that San - ta's com - ing, And soon will be here. Good

Bm7
A7
D7
G
tid - ings we bring to you and your kin. Good
D7
G
C
D7
G
tid - ings for Christ - mas and a hap - py New Year. We
C
E7
A7
D
wish you a Mer - ry Christ - mas, We wish you a Mer - ry Christ - mas, We
B7
Em
G/B
C
D7
G
wish you a Mer - ry Christ - mas, and a hap - py New Year.

# WE THREE KINGS OF ORIENT ARE

Words and Music by
JOHN H. HOPKINS, JR.

Em
D7
G
C
star. O star of won - der, star of
G
C
night, Star with roy - al beau - ty
G
Em
D
G
C
G
bright, West - ward lead - ing, still pro -
D
G
C
G
ceed - ing, Guide us to thy per - fect light.

# WELSH CAROL

Words by PASTOR K.E. ROBERTS
Traditional Welsh Carol

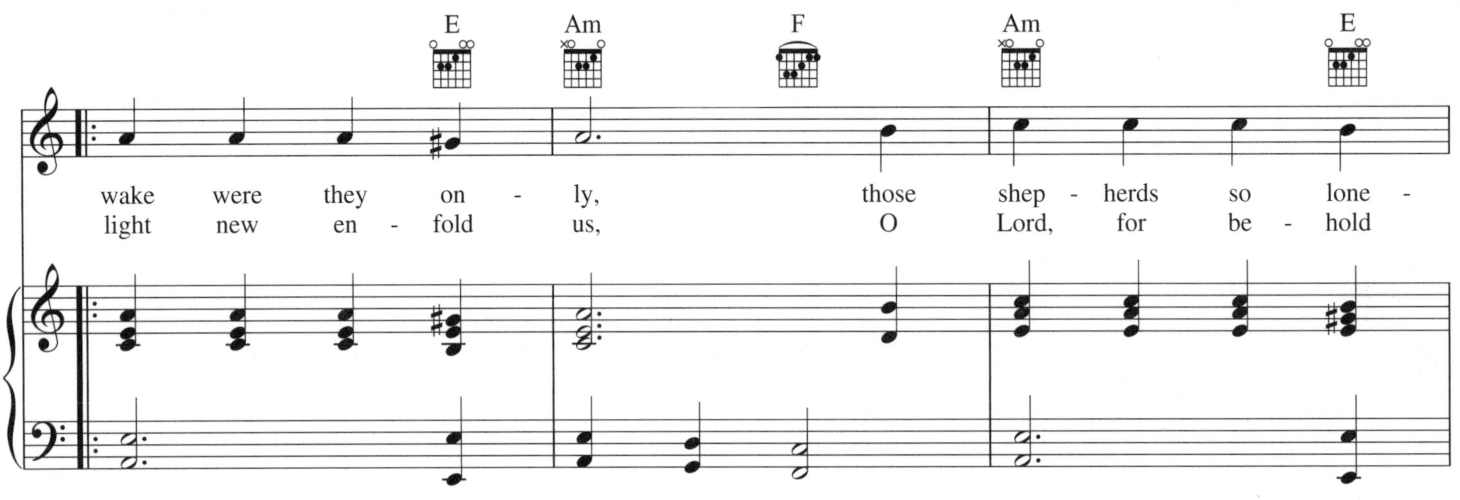


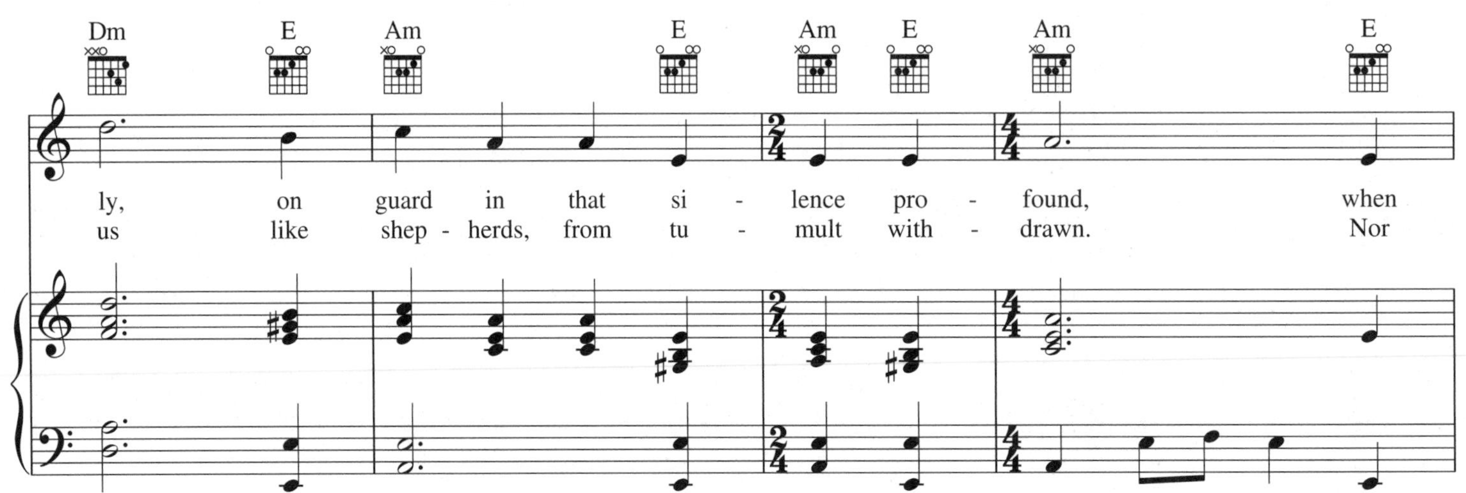

Am E Am F G Am E
col - or had fad - ed, when night - time had shad -
heav - ing, nor see - ing, all oth - er care flee -
Dm E Am E Am E
ed, their sens - es from sight and from
ing, we wait the in - ef - fa - ble
Am G7 C
sound. Lo, then broke the won -
dawn. O Spir - it all - know -
G E Am E
der, then drift - ed a - sun - der the
ing, Thou source o - ver - flow - ing, O

Am E Dm Am E
veils from the splen - dor of God, when
move in the dark - ness a - round, that
Am E Am E Am E
light from the Ho - ly, came down to the low -
sight may be in us, true hear - ing to win
Dm E Am E Am E
ly, and heav'n to the earth that they
us, glad tid - ings where Christ may be
1 Am
trod. May
2 Am
found.

# WHAT CHILD IS THIS?

Words by WILLIAM C. DIX
16th Century English Melody

Em Am Em
ing? Whom an - gels greet with
ing? Good Chris - tian, fear; for
Him. The King of kings sal -
F♯m Bm C Bm Am
an - thems sweet while shep - herds
sin - ners here the si - lent
va - tion brings, let bow - ing
B7 E A E G
watch are keep - ing?
Word is plead - ing.
hearts en - throne Him.
This,
F♯m Bm Em
this is Christ the King, whom shep - herds

F#7
B
B7
guard and an - gels sing:
G
F#m
Haste, haste to bring Him
Bm
C
B7
laud, the Babe, the Son of
1, 2
Am
Em
3
E
Mar - y. Why So
Mar - y.

# WEXFORD CAROL

Traditional Irish Carol

*Additional Lyrics*

3. Near Bethlehem did shepherds keep
Their flocks of lambs and feeding sheep;
To whom God's angels did appear,
Which put the shepherds in great fear.
"Prepare and go," the angels said,
"To Bethlehem, be not afraid;
For there you'll find this happy morn
A princely Babe, sweet Jesus born."

4. With thankful heart and joyful mind,
The shepherds went, the Babe to find;
And as God's angel had foretold,
They did our Savior Christ behold.
Within a manger He was laid,
And by His side, the virgin maid,
Attending on the Lord of life,
Who came to earth to end all strife.

5. There were three wise men from afar,
Directed by a glorious star;
And on they wandered night and day,
Until they came where Jesus lay.
And when they came unto that place
Where our beloved Messiah was,
They humbly cast them at His feet,
With gifts of gold and incense sweet.

# WHEN CHRIST WAS BORN OF MARY FREE

Music by ARTHUR H. BROWN
Traditional Text, 15th Century

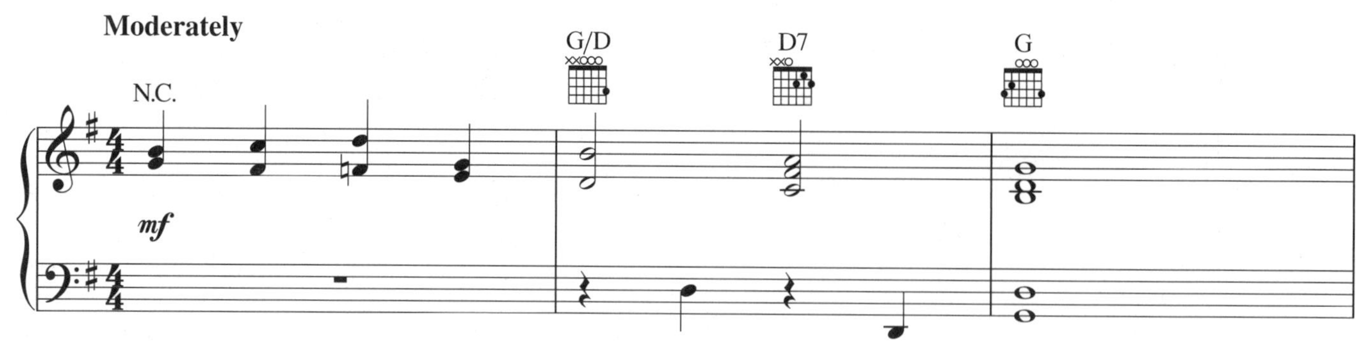


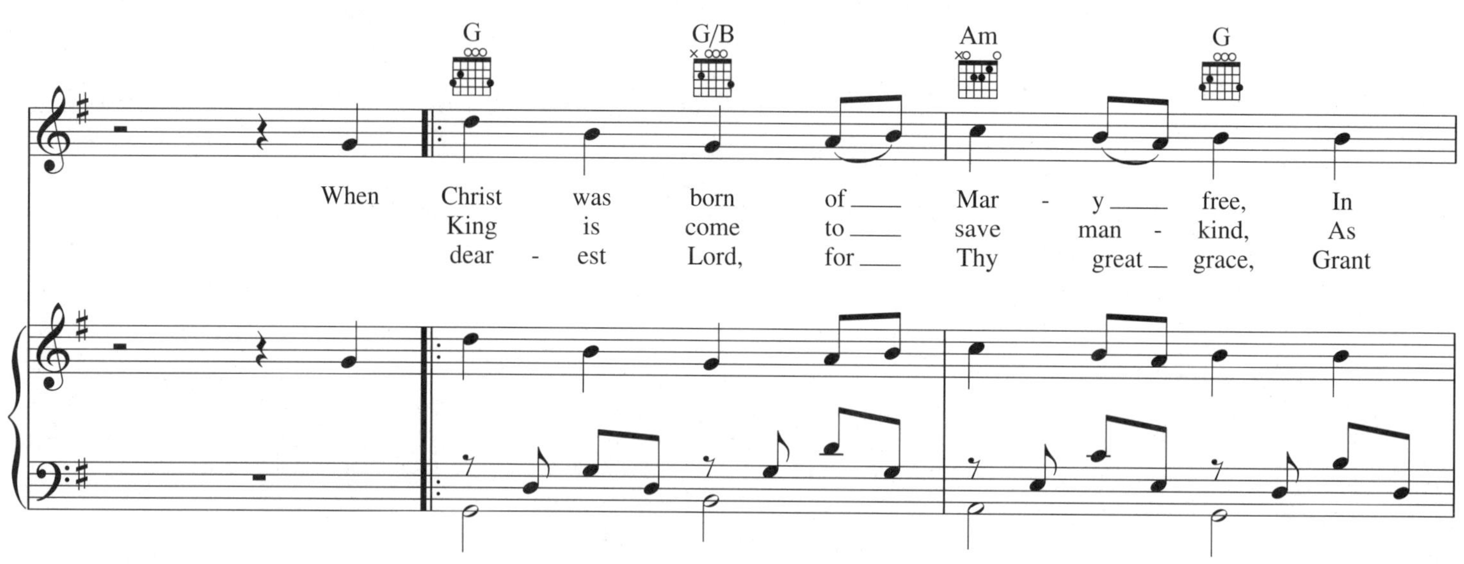


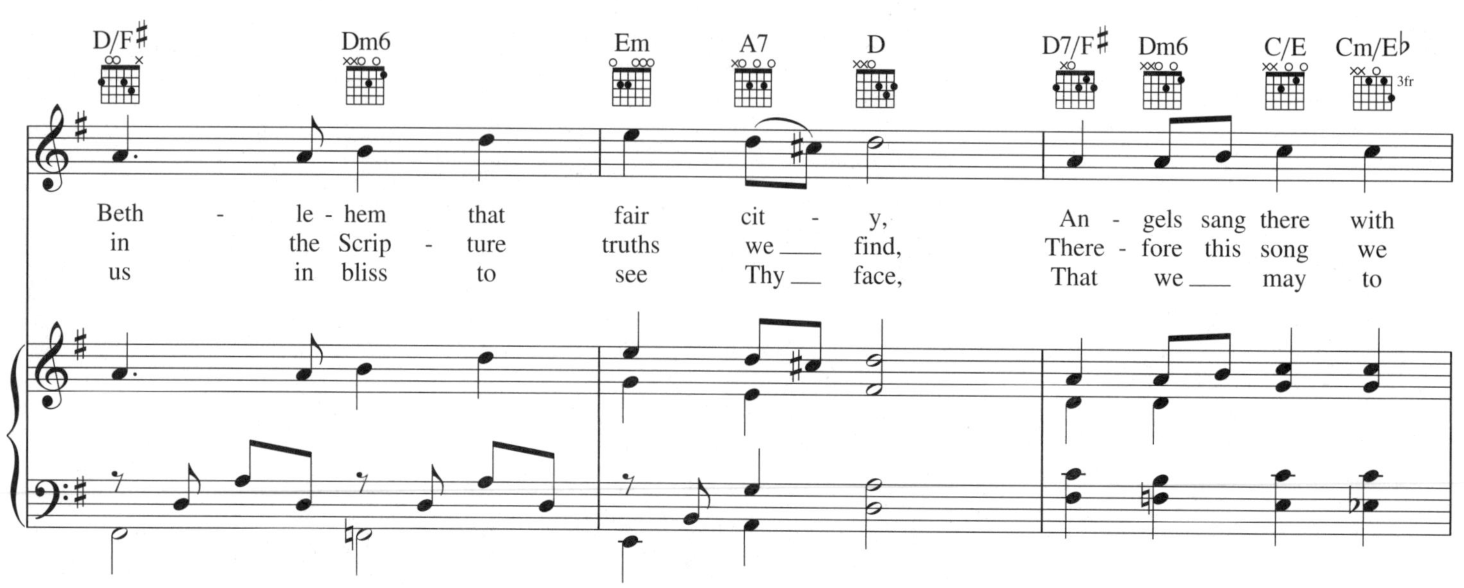

G/D
Cm6
3fr
G/B
G/D
D7
G
mirth and glee:
have in mind:
Thy sol - ace,
In ex - cel - sis glo - ri - a.
G/B
C
G/B
C6
Am
In ex - cel - sis glo - ri - a,
In ex - cel - sis
G
D7
G
G/B
Em7
F6
D7/F♯
glo - ri - a,
In ex - cel - sis glo - ri - a,
G
G/D
C♯m7♭5
4fr
1, 2
G/D
D7
G
3
G/D
D7
G
In ex - cel - sis glo - ri - a.
The
Then,
glo - ri - a.

# WHILE SHEPHERDS WATCHED THEIR FLOCKS

Words by NAHUM TATE
Music by GEORGE FRIDERIC HANDEL

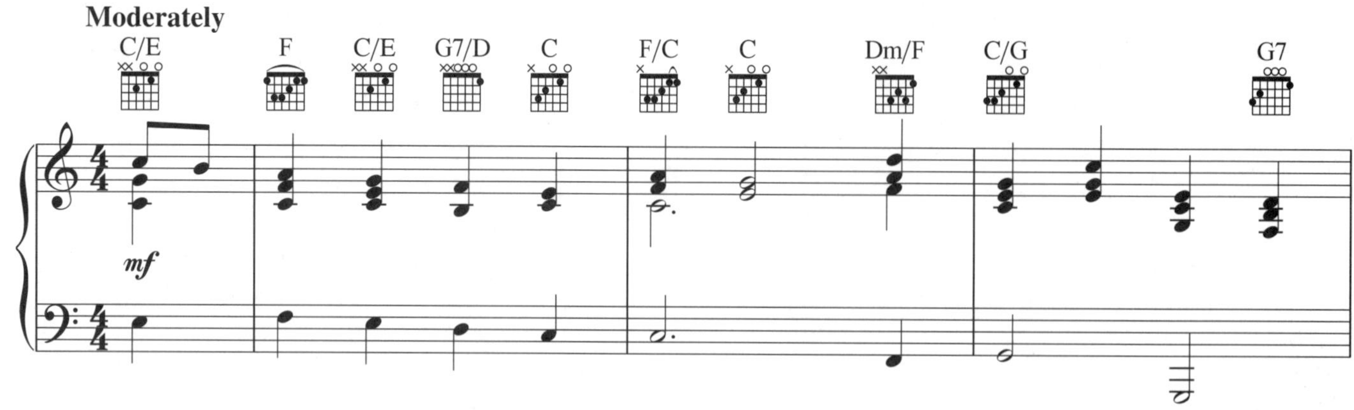


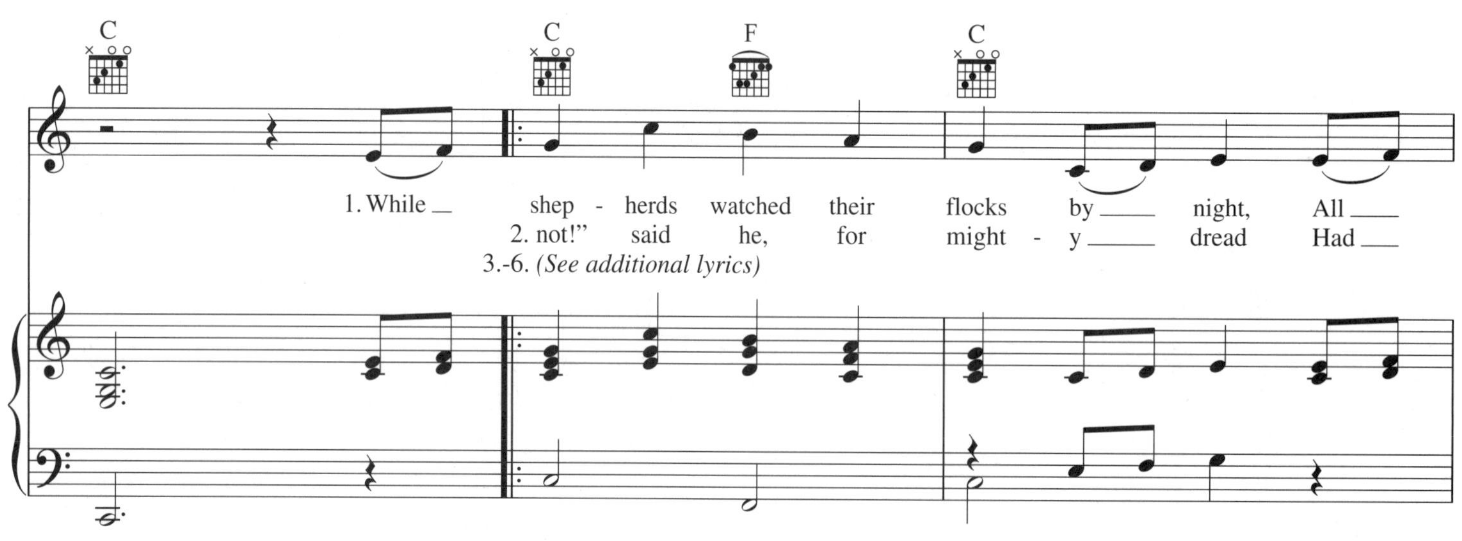

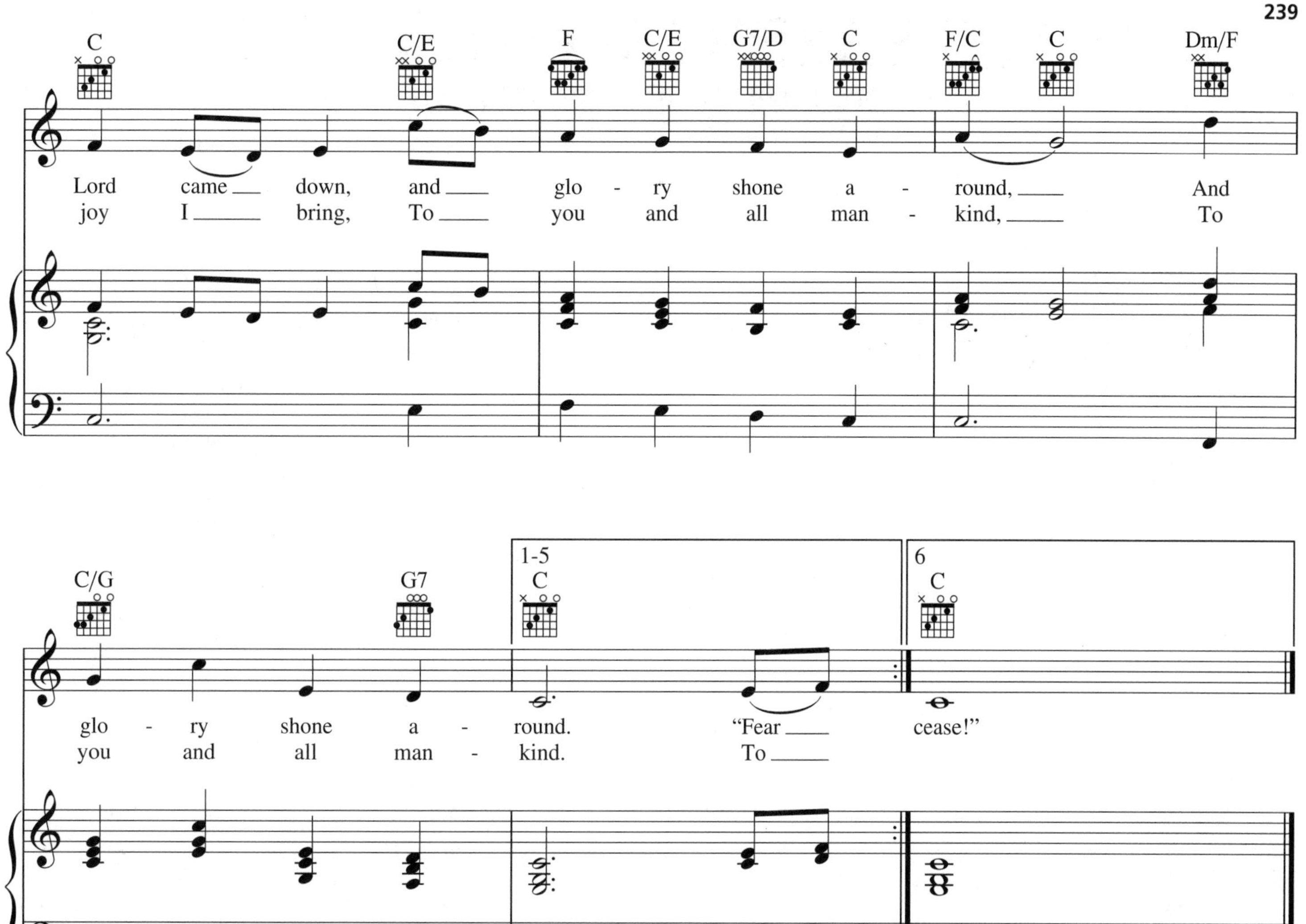


*Additional Lyrics*

3. To you, in David's town this day,
   Is born of David's line,
   The Savior, who is Christ the Lord;
   And this shall be the sign,
   And this shall be the sign:

4. The heavenly Babe you there shall find
   To human view displayed,
   All meanly wrapped in swathing bands,
   And in a manger laid,
   And in a manger laid."

5. Thus spake the seraph; and forthwith
   Appeared a shining throng
   Of angels praising God on high,
   Who thus addressed their song,
   Who thus addressed their song:

6. "All glory be to God on high,
   And to the earth be peace;
   Good will henceforth from heav'n to men,
   Begin and never cease,
   Begin and never cease!"

# YA VIENE LA VIEJA
## (Come, My Dear Old Woman)

Traditional Spanish Carol

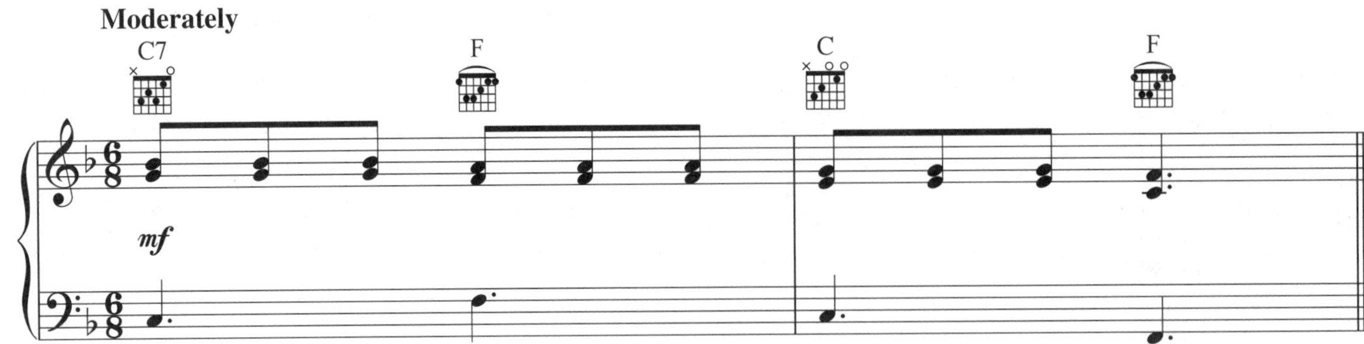


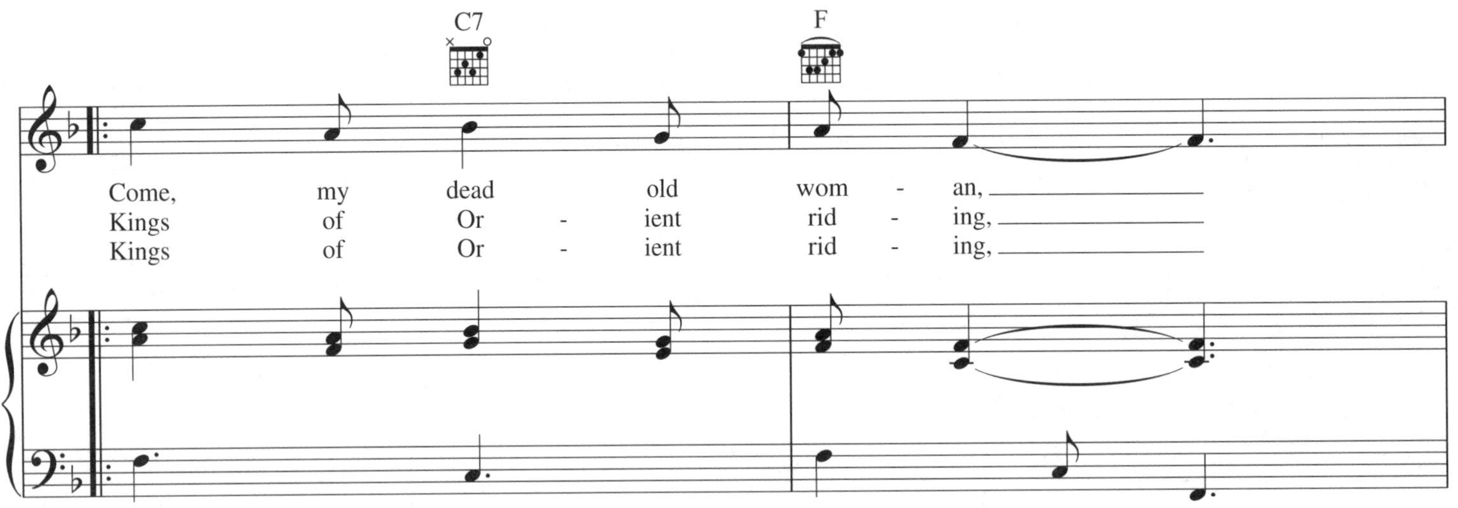


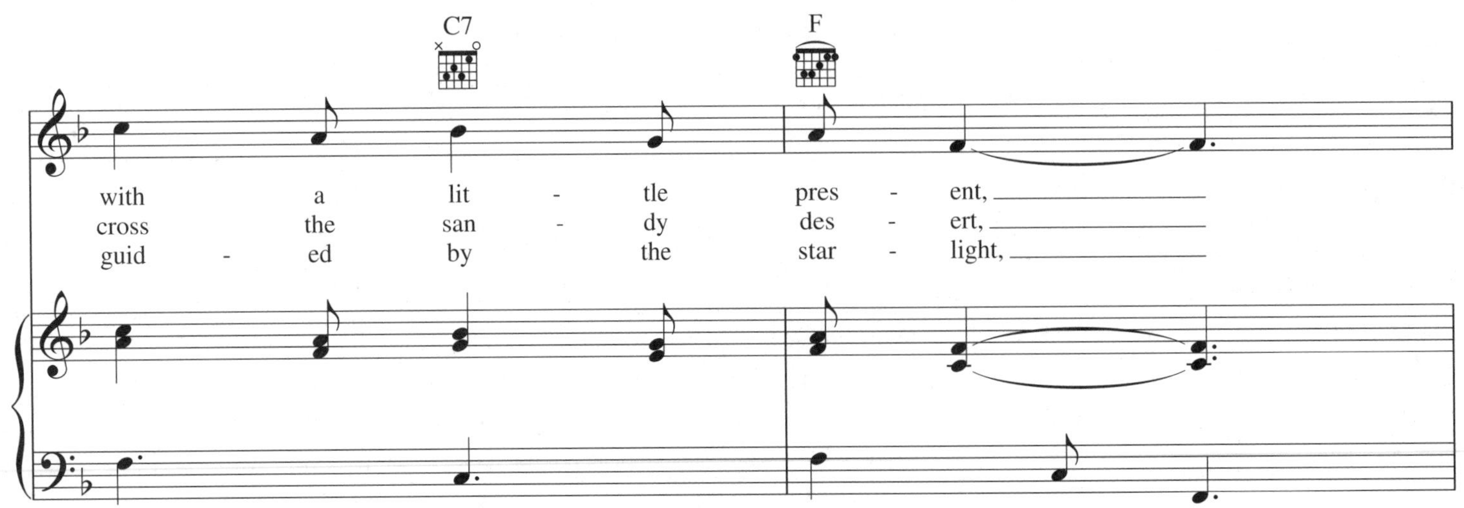

E♭
3fr
F
that you love so dear - ly.
bring - ing to the Chi - ld,
bring - ing to the Chi - ld,
C7
F
C7
Of - fer it to Je - sus.
wine and cook - ies sweet.
gifts of love to - night.
We're weav - ing a
F
C7
F
C7
gar - ment of green lem - on leaves for sweet Vir - gin
1, 2
3
F
C7
F
F
Mar - y, the Moth - er of God!
God!

# WINDS THROUGH THE OLIVE TREES

19th Century American Carol

# YULETIDE IS HERE AGAIN

Traditional Swedish Dance Carol